BERNARD SHAW, DIRECTOR

Bernard Shaw, Director

BERNARD F. DUKORE

London
GEORGE ALLEN & UNWIN LTD
RUSKIN HOUSE · MUSEUM STREET

FIRST PUBLISHED IN 1971

© Bernard F. Dukore, 1971

ISBN 0 04 928023 6

PRINTED IN GREAT BRITAIN
in 12 point Fournier
BY WILLMER BROTHERS LIMITED, BIRKENHEAD

To Joyce

ACKNOWLEDGMENTS

For permission to quote from Shaw's published and unpublished work, I am grateful to the Public Trustee and the Society of Authors. For their help in locating and for their permission to quote from works by Shaw in their collections, my sincere thanks go to The Trustees of the British Museum; the University Library of the University of California at Los Angeles; the Cornell University Library; Houghton Library, Harvard College; the Henry W. and Albert A. Berg Collection and also the Manuscript Division, both of The New York Public Library, Astor, Lenox, and Tilden Foundations; the University of North Carolina Library; the Academic Center Library, University of Texas at Austin; the Victoria and Albert Museum; and the Yale University Library. I should also like to thank Norman Philbrick for making available to me unpublished Shavian letters in his private library.

It is a pleasure to acknowledge my obligation to colleagues and friends in the theatre and academe, and also at home. For their generous assistance, I owe thanks to Dame Sybil Thorndike, Wendy Hiller, and Ronald Gow. I am beholden to Professor Sidney P. Albert for our hours of dialogue on Shaw's plays in general and on my production of *Major Barbara* in particular. For Professor Ruby Cohn's constructive advice upon reading an early draft I am most grateful. For detailed comments on the final draft and for valuable suggestions, I am greatly indebted to my wife Joyce. I hope I have profited from their criticisms.

CONTENTS

ILLUSTRATIONS

INTRODUCTION

Bernard Shaw devoted many years of his life to the art of play directing. Not only was he a director of considerable experience, he was extremely good, and his practices, moreover, anticipated those of modern directors. As early as the 1890s, when he was relatively inexperienced, his writings vividly demonstrated a knowledge of theatre practice. Blaming Ellen Terry for making it appear that another actor had fluffed his lines, he explained why she was probably at fault: 'I suppose you didnt give him his cue, and he waited long enough to be detected before he made up his mind that he was not going to get it.'[1] In his weekly theatre criticisms for the *Saturday Review*, backstage terminology spiced his comments on stagecraft. He reprimanded one director, for instance, for having 'so far neglected the ancient counsel to "jine his flats" as to leave a gap in the roof . . .'.[2] These examples could easily be multiplied. As Shaw remarked in an uncharacteristic understatement, 'I am not a dreamer who doesnt understand the practical exigencies of the stage . . .'.[3]

Understanding, however, is different from experience. Shaw had both. His knowledge of 'the practical exigencies of the stage' derived from several sources. By 1895, he had written four plays, started a fifth, and participated in the London productions of two – as supervising author of *Widowers' Houses* and as director of *Arms and the Man*.[4] In the years that followed his 1894 pro-

[1] Letter to Ellen Terry, April 16, 1897, in *Ellen Terry and Bernard Shaw: A Correspondence*, ed. Christopher St John (New York: The Fountain Press, 1931), p. 150 (hereafter cited as *Terry-Shaw*). Throughout I reproduce Shaw's idiosyncratic punctuation and spelling. He eliminates the apostrophe from such words as *don't*, *doesn't*, and *they'll*, although *I'll* remains the same. *Show* becomes *shew*, and *Shakespeare* may be *Shakespear* or *Shakspere*.

[2] Bernard Shaw, *Our Theatres in the Nineties* (London: Constable Standard Edition, 1931), III, 264. Unless otherwise indicated, quotations from Shaw's published writings are from the Standard Edition of the Works of Bernard Shaw, which Constable published in London beginning in 1931. Following the initial citation to a given work, references to works by Shaw will include only the title and relevant page numbers.

[3] Letter to Ellen Terry, Sept. 14, 1897, in *Terry-Shaw*, p. 207.

[4] Raymond Mander and Joe Mitchenson, *Theatrical Companion to Shaw* (London: Rockliff, 1954), pp. 21, 36.

duction of *Arms and the Man*, he directed many plays. At the Court Theatre, under the management of J. E. Vedrenne and Granville Barker, Shaw was as actively and successfully engaged in directing his plays as he was in writing them. By the end of the First World War, he was a seasoned director as well as an experienced playwright.

When a major dramatist expends so much of his creative energies on the art and craft of play production, it becomes mandatory to examine just what he did. Surprisingly, there has been little attempt to do so. Eight pages of Raymond Mander and Joe Mitchenson's *Theatrical Companion to Shaw* are devoted to accounts by Dame Sybil Thorndike and Sir Lewis Casson of Shaw as director; Archibald Henderson's major biography *George Bernard Shaw: Man of the Century* gives only twenty of its almost one thousand pages to this topic; Eric Bentley comments on 'Shaw and the Actors' in a thirteen-page appendix to the 1957 edition of his *Bernard Shaw;* and William A. Armstrong has written a fifteen-page article on Shaw as director.[5] Heretofore, there has been no full-length treatment of the subject.

This book studies Shaw as artist of the theatre, mainly from the point of view of director (or producer, as the director is called in England). My primary concern is not Shaw's playwriting practices or his theories of playwriting, but rather his ideas and methods of putting the play on the stage. The subject of the initial chapter is Shaw's background and experiences in the theatre before he began to direct plays. Following this chapter, the book divides into different aspects of play directing and various areas with which the director is concerned. My procedure is to analyse first Shaw's theoretical and critical pronouncements,

[5] Mander and Mitchenson, *Theatrical Companion to Shaw*, pp. 11-18; Archibald Henderson, *George Bernard Shaw: Man of the Century* (New York: Appleton-Century-Crofts, 1956), pp. 669–88; Eric Bentley, *Bernard Shaw, 1856–1950* (New York: New Directions, 1957), pp. 220–32; William A. Armstrong, 'George Bernard Shaw: The Playwright as Producer', *Modern Drama*, VIII (February 1966), 347–61. During Shaw's lifetime, several actors received titles. I shall refer to them by their titles only if they had these titles at the time of reference. Thus, the actress is Sybil Thorndike when she played the title role in *Saint Joan*, but Dame Sybil Thorndike when she wrote the article in Mander and Mitchenson.

and then his practices. For the theory-criticism, my sources are Shaw's theatre and opera reviews, essays, letters, prefaces and the like. In these, he frequently refers to the plays of Shakespeare and Ibsen. The practical problems centre almost exclusively on his own plays. Sources of this information are chiefly notes which Shaw made during rehearsals. In addition, I use Shaw's letters to various actors. Where possible (and in most cases it is possible) I choose examples from Shaw's comments on productions of his better-known plays rather than of his less well-known plays: *Caesar and Cleopatra* and *Pygmalion,* for instance, rather than *Augustus Does His Bit* and *The Inca of Perusalem*. Although Shaw did not direct plays by other authors, he did on a few occasions advise on their production, and I have used certain of these comments in order to demonstrate his consistent approach.

Shaw's basic concern is the actor, who is the major element of production. In working with actors, he employed virtually all of the techniques that a modern director might use – ranging from animal imagery to mechanical, technical instruction. But Shaw was a director, not merely an acting coach. He supervised every element of production: scenery (construction and painting, as well as design), lighting, costuming, make-up – even business and house management.

Is this so unusual? What may surprise the reader is not that Shaw's practice was different from that of the modern director but that it was similar. His practice was completely harmonious with the twentieth-century tradition of the director as guiding artist in the production of a play. However, in 1894, when Shaw began to direct plays, this tradition had not yet been established. In late nineteenth-century London, the tradition was that of the actor-manager: a star actor supervising his satellite company. Unity of production under the guidance of a director, a common-place idea today, was not at all commonplace in England in the late nineteenth century. A supervising, powerful figure who was not a star actor was rare; the authoritarian play-directing of an author – W. S. Gilbert, for example – was unusual. For that matter, play production under the leadership of a strong director was exceptional on the Continent as well as in England. The Meiningen Company (1874–90) was outside then-current theatrical traditions. The Moscow Art Theatre, which at its start had a strong director guiding the actors, was organized in 1898, four years after Shaw's directorial debut. Gordon Craig's influential pronouncements advocating unity of production under the supervision of a single directing mind did not appear until 1905, when *The Art of the Theatre* was published – eleven years after Shaw directed *Arms and the Man*. Shaw's work as a director is therefore important for three reasons: first, because he is a major playwright who directed his own works; second, because he was a good director; and third, because he is an early example of the modern idea of the director as guiding artist in the production of a play.

I
Theatre Background and Experience

By the time he was ten years old, says Shaw, he was 'saturated' with both Shakespeare and the Bible. As a child, he adored the theatre. On his first visit he saw Tom Taylor's *Plot and Passion*, which was followed by a full-length Christmas pantomime, *Puss in Boots*, whose attractions included a fairy queen, a policeman shooting a gun, and a disappearance through a grave-trap.[1] In his three-volume collection of theatre reviews, *Our Theatres in the Nineties*, there are numerous references to plays and performances which he probably saw in Dublin, as well as an explicit statement that he had ten years' playgoing experience before moving to London.[2]

Growing up in Dublin, Shaw attended the Theatre Royal, the Gaiety, and the Queen's, where he saw tragedies and melodramas, high comedies and farces, musical extravaganzas and Christmas pantomimes – virtually every type of play. His reminiscences include comments on the scenery and performances, for he was attentive not only to the plays themselves but also to the manner in which they were produced. In these theatres, stock scenery served for each play; staging techniques included closing flats, the descent of sky borders and front-scenes, wings-and-grooves, and illumination by coal-gas; and resident stock-companies supported such visiting stars as Charles Mathews, John Hare, Dion Boucicault, Kate Bateman, Edward Sothern, and Barry Sullivan.[3] Sullivan – whose repertoire featured *Richard III*,

---

1 Henderson, *Shaw*, pp. 30–31, 39.
2 *Our Theatres in the Nineties*, I, 280.
3 Henderson, *Shaw*, pp. 40–1; *Shaw on Theatre*, ed. E. J. West (New York: Hill and Wang, 1959), p. 161; Terry-Shaw, p. xviii; Martin Meisel, *Shaw and the Nineteenth-Century Theater* (Princeton, N.J.: Princeton University Press, 1963), p. 14.

Hamlet, Macbeth, Othello, and *Richelieu* – made so deep an impression on young Shaw that as late as 1947 he vividly described details of Sullivan's athletic performance of Richard III.[4]

Not only did Shaw attend the professional theatre in Dublin, he also participated in amateur theatricals. At the Dublin English Scientific and Commercial Day School, which he entered at the age of thirteen, he and Matthew Edward McNulty organized a drama club that aimed to produce the major works of Shakespeare. The results were disastrous. For their first production, *Macbeth,* none of the actors memorized his lines, and the performance collapsed after twenty minutes when the prompter gave up. In the club's second and final effort, *Hamlet,* Shaw tiptoed on stage as Ophelia and used a falsetto voice that turned the tragedy into a comedy.[5]

His early experience with amateur theatricals included the operatic stage, for his mother became involved with George John Vandeleur Lee, voice teacher and conductor, whose enthusiasms included opera. In the two years between April 1871 and March 1873, Lee produced and conducted a series of amateur operas in which Shaw's mother performed. She played Azucena in Verdi's *Il Trovatore,* Donna Anna in Mozart's *Don Giovanni,* Margaret in Gounod's *Faust,* and the title role in Donizetti's *Lucrezia Borgia.* Since all of these operas were rehearsed at home, Shaw 'whistled and sang them from the first bar to the last . . .'. During this period Lee extended his range from opera to theatre. Merging his Amateur Musical Society with another Dublin amateur group, the Operatic and Dramatic Society, he produced Racine's *Athalie* in 1872.[6] The closeness of the relationship between Lee and the Shaw household, as well as the evidence of Shaw's letter,

---

[4] *Shaw on Theatre,* p. 274; for confirming opinions, written when Shaw was much younger, see *Terry-Shaw,* p. xxii; *Our Theaters in the Nineties,* I, 182–4, 271–3. Although one would ordinarily question the accuracy of a nonagenarian's account of a production he saw when he was a teenager, Shaw's 1947 description of Sullivan is in no way incompatible with those he gave in 1929 and in 1895.

[5] B. C. Rosset, *Shaw of Dublin: The Formative Years* (University Park: Pennsylvania State University Press, 1964), pp. 198–9.

[6] Letter to Archibald Henderson, Jan. 17, 1905, in Henderson, *Shaw,* pp. 36–7; Rosset, *Shaw of Dublin,* pp. 228–36.

make it appear likely that at the very least Shaw attended rehearsals of Lee's Dublin productions.

In 1873 Lee and Mrs Shaw moved to London, and three years later, young Shaw followed. In London, Lee organized a musical society called The Troubadours, which performed operas. After Mrs Shaw ended her association with Lee, her son occasionally assumed her role of piano accompanist during rehearsals and once (in 1881) during the actual performance. Prior to 1883, he assisted Lee in productions of *Faust, Il Trovatore, Don Giovanni*, and Gilbert and Sullivan's *Patience* and *Pinafore*. Apart from piano accompaniment, we do not know the specific nature of Shaw's contribution to Lee's operatic ventures, though on at least one occasion Lee asked him to prepare press releases.[7] As far as we know, none of the contributions was on the actor's side of the footlights.

On a few occasions Shaw did act in the nonmusical theatre. He played Stratton Strawless in a benefit performance of *Alone*, by Palgrave Simpson and Herman Merivale, which the Socialist League presented on January 30, 1885. The cast included Edward Aveling (the model for the unscrupulous artist Dubedat in *The Doctor's Dilemma*), Eleanor Marx Aveling (Karl Marx's daughter and Aveling's mistress), and May Morris (William Morris' daughter).[8] Shaw also played a photographer in an amateur performance at William Morris' house during one of the Socialist League's soirées, and he was Krogstad in a drawingroom performance of Ibsen's *A Doll's House*, with Eleanor Marx Aveling as Nora Helmer.[9] These amateur performances may have given him a nodding acquaintance with the problems of the actor and of play production, but Shaw certainly did not gain a great deal of directing experience as an actor.

Some of the knowledge and background that Shaw brought to his directing he gained as a critic. Although he was not a regular play reviewer until *after* his directorial debut in 1894 – writing

7 Rosset, *Shaw of Dublin*, pp. 329–33.

8 Bernard Shaw, *Collected Letters*, 1874–1897, ed. Dan H. Laurence (New York: Dodd, Mead, 1965), p. 115 and plate facing p. 115.

9 Henderson, *Shaw*, p. 669.

weekly theatre criticisms in the *Saturday Review* during the years 1895-98 – he was, during the 1880s and early 1890s, a critic of art and music. In both capacities his directorial eyes and ears were being developed. As an art critic, he dealt with composition, colour, emphasis, and balance. This background not only helped Shaw the director to supervise the scenery for his productions, it also helped him to visualize the composition and movement of the actors within that scenery. As a music critic evaluating the staging of operas, he analysed directing, acting, scenery, lighting, costuming, and make-up – all of the aspects of play production with which he would soon be concerned as a director.

Until his own plays were staged, however, Shaw did not become seriously involved with the actual business of play production. On December 9, 1892, J. T. Grein's Independent Theatre Society performed *Widowers' Houses*, Shaw's first play. Five days later he confided to Charles Charrington: 'I have spent so much time at rehearsal that I am stark ruined, and am ruefully asking myself whether a continental trip for my health would not have been far more economical than all this theatrical glory.'[10] Herman de Lange received directing credit for the production that occasioned this lament, and one may infer that Shaw functioned as supervising author.

The next London production of a Shaw play (his first on the West End) was *Arms and the Man*, which he himself directed in 1894. Between 1894 and 1924, according to Raymond Mander and Joe Mitchenson, Shaw directed nineteen productions of his plays and codirected four others (two productions of *Caesar and Cleopatra* with Forbes Robertson, *Heartbreak House* with J. B. Fagan, and *Saint Joan* with Lewis Casson). Even when someone else is given credit for having directed the early plays, Mander and Mitchenson assert, 'one may be certain that G.B.S. was behind him at rehearsals'.[11] This statement is verified by the thousands of notes Shaw made during rehearsals of plays for which others are listed as directors: for example, Arnold Daly's 1911 production

[10] Letter to Charles Charrington, Dec. 14, 1892, in *Collected Letters*, p. 372.
[11] Mander and Mitchenson, *Theatrical Companion to Shaw*, p. 10.

of *Arms and the Man,* and Robert Loraine's 1919 production of the same play.[12] During the famous 'Vedrenne-Barker seasons' at the Court Theatre, from 1904 to 1907, Shaw was one of the Court's directors as well as its 'house playwright'. He claims, and Granville Barker admits, that even though Barker is credited with having staged most of Shaw's plays, Shaw himself was responsible for their direction.[13]

At the Court, Shaw and Barker eliminated artificial acting in favour of what Desmond MacCarthy calls 'actuality in gesture, diction, and sentiment'. Audiences saw realistic, believable performances, dedicated to the requirements of the role rather than to the exhibition of an actor's bag of tricks. And they saw ensemble acting, which was very different from the practice at other theatres. At the Court, a performer with a major part in one play might appear in a walk-on in another. Edmund Gwenn, for instance, played the important role of Enry Straker, Tanner's chauffeur in *Man and Superman,* and the minor role of Bilton, custodian of the gun-cotton shed in the last act of *Major Barbara.* Devotion to the ensemble and to the requirements of the play, rather than to self-display, led to far better acting than otherwise would have been the case. 'At the Court', MacCarthy declared, 'the acting pleased from the first. People began to say that the English could act after all, and that London must be full of intelligent actors, of whom nobody had ever heard. Yet, strange to say, these actors, when they appeared in other plays on other boards, seemed to sink again to normal insignificance.'[14] Under the guidance of Shaw and Barker, productions at the Court were, according to MacCarthy, 'remarkable enough to challenge the highest standards . . . I should not have felt so keenly when

12 Rehearsal notes: *Arms and the Man:* 1911, Academic Center Library, University of Texas, Austin (hereafter cited as Texas), and British Museum, Add. 50644; 1919, Burgunder Collection, Cornell University Library, Ithaca, N.Y. (hereafter cited as Burgunder Collection).

13 Bernard Shaw, 'Granville-Barker', *Drama,* n.s., III (Winter 1946), 10; Barker's admission was made in a testimonial speech, quoted in *Desmond MacCarthy's The Court Theatre 1904–1907: A Commentary and Criticism,* ed. Stanley Weintraub (Coral Gables, Fla: University of Miami Press, 1966), p. 164.

14 *Desmond MacCarthy's The Court Theatre,* pp. 12–14.

anything was lacking in their performances had they not shown me at the same time to what pitch of excellence it is possible to attain'.[15]

In 'The Art of Rehearsal' (1922), Shaw described directing as 'hard work' because of the 'incessant strain on one's attention (the actors have their exits and rests; but the producer is hard at it all the time), the social effort of keeping up everyone's spirits in view of a great event, [and] the dryness of the previous study of the mechanical details . . .'. He called it a 'grind . . . which I face with greater reluctance as I grow older . . .'.[16] But he did face it, for he consistently maintained that 'the art of producing plays . . . is as much in my profession as writing them',[17] and that the 'most desirable director of a play is the author'. The most undesirable director, on the other hand, was the actor when that actor was also performing in the production. One or both, he maintained, was bound to suffer. 'Producing kills acting: an actor's part dies if he is watching the others critically. You cannot conduct an orchestra and play the drum at the same concert.'[18]

What did Shaw do when he 'conducted his orchestra'? To answer this, we must first answer two related questions: What is the purpose of 'conducting'? Does the process of 'conducting' begin when the 'conductor' meets the 'orchestra' at rehearsal? The subjects of the next chapter are Shaw's ideas of the purposes of play directing and the nature of the director's prerehearsal work.

15 *Ibid.*, p. 103.

16 *Shaw on Theatre*, p. 158.

17 Letter to Louis Wilkinson, Dec. 6, 1909, in Frank Harris, *Bernard Shaw* (Garden City, N.Y.: Garden City Publishing Co., 1931), p. 254.

18 *Shaw on Theatre*, pp. 266, 279.

II

The Director:
Goals and Groundwork

THE DIRECTOR'S AIMS

In Shaw's opinion, 'The director, having considered the play, and decided to undertake the job of directing it, has no further concern with its literary merits or its doctrine (if any)'. If a director's notes contain such statements as ' "Shew influence of Kierkegaard on Ibsen in this scene", or "The Oedipus complex must be very apparent here. Discuss with the Queen", the sooner he is packed out of the theatre and replaced the better'. If, on the other hand, he has noted 'Ears too red', 'Further up to make room for X', 'Mariar Ann', 'Contrast', 'Unladylike: keep knees together', 'More dialogue to give them time to get off', 'Tibbeeyrnottibee-that iz' (meaning that Hamlet should say, 'To be? Or NOT to be? THAT is the question'), 'chaste tars' (meaning that Othello should not slur 'chaste stars'), and the like, then the director knows his business.[1] But these notes represent means, not ends. In 'The Art of Rehearsal', Shaw announced one of the director's aims: 'The beginning and end of the business [of play production] from the author's point of view is the art of making the audience believe that real things are happening to real people.'[2]

This was a Shavian critical criterion of long standing. As a music critic, using the pen name Corno di Bassetto, he implored the opera impresario Augustus Harris to remove the 'barnstorming absurdities' of the operatic stage:

[Harris] should go to his singers and say gently 'Do not saw the air thus. You think yourselves fine fellows when you do it; but the public thinks you idiots. The English nation, among

1 *Shaw on Theatre*, pp. 279, 284.
2 *Ibid.*, p, 153.

whom I am a councillor, no longer supposes that attitudinizing is acting. Neither would I have you suppose that all native young men wear dove-colored tights, and have pink cheeks with little moustaches. Nor is it the case that all men with grown-up daughters have long white beards reaching to the waist, or that they walk totteringly with staves, raising hands and eyes to heaven whenever they offer an observation. The daughters of Albion do not, when in distress, leave off wearing bonnets in the open air, assume mourning, keep their hands continually on their hearts, and stagger and flop about like decapitated geese.' And so on. Harris's advice to the opera singers would become more celebrated than Hamlet's to the players.[3]

As theatre critic for the *Saturday Review*, Shaw similarly satirized unrealistic staging and stereotyped acting. In 1897 he called a production of *John Gabriel Borkman* 'old fashioned' because it conceived the play as a conventional tragedy and ignored realistic behaviour. This production concept, he complained,

> lends itself to people talking at each other rhetorically from opposite sides of the stage, taking long sweeping walks up to their 'points', striking attitudes . . . with an artificiality which, instead of being concealed, is not only disclosed but insisted on, and being affected in all their joints by emotions which a fine comedian conveys by the faintest possible inflexion of tone or eyebrow.[4]

The basis of such complaints was that the directors ignored what Shaw believed to be the fundamental aim of play production: '. . . making the audience believe that real things are happening to real people'.

An important aspect of this goal of credibility – indeed, its basis, according to Shaw – is the desire of the author. Not only

---

[3] Bernard Shaw, *London Music in 1888–89 As Heard by Corno di Bassetto (Later Known as Bernard Shaw) with Some Further Autobiographical Particulars*, pp. 99–100 (hereafter cited as *London Music*).

[4] *Our Theatres in the Nineties*, III, 124.

must the director arrange the stage to produce an illusion of reality, he must also produce the particular illusion intended by by the author.[5] The 'real people' are the people the author created, and the real things happen in the world he created. Contributing to the illusion are the duration of the play, the relationship between stage and auditorium, and the nature of the scenic effects. Shaw insisted that a play should be neither shorter nor longer than its author intended, nor should its scenes be rearranged. The distance between the stage and the spectators should not place the actors in a less intimate relationship to the audience than the author planned – which is what happens, for example, when a Shakespearean play is transferred from the platform stage to behind the proscenium arch. He further insisted that the attention of the spectators not be 'divided and distracted by quantities of furniture and appointments greatly in excess of the author's demands', and that neither directors nor actors 'take advantage of modern contrivances to make effects that the author never contemplated . . .'.[6]

Another major goal of the director concerns the actors. Shaw recalls having asked William Reed 'whether he agreed with Wagner that the first duty of a conductor is to give the right time to the band. "No," said he. "The first duty of a conductor is to let the band play." ' Agreeing with this precept, Shaw applied it to the theatre: 'The perfect producer lets his actors act; and is their helper at need and not their dictator. The hint is meant specially for producers who have begun as actors. They are the first instead of the last to forget it.'[7] He condemned Henry Irving for 'not allowing his company to act. He worked hard to make them do what he wanted for his own effects; but if they tried to make independent effects of their own, he did not hesitate to spoil them by tricks of stage management.' On the other hand, he praised Herbert Beerbohm Tree for giving members of his company 'as big a chance as himself in the production . . . he

5 Bernard Shaw, *Music in London, 1890–1894*, I, 247.

6 Letter to Joseph Harker, on date, in Joseph Harker, *Studio and Stage* (London: Nisbet, 1924), p. 189.

7 *Shaw on Theatre*, p. 267.

surrounds himself with counter-attractions and lets them play him off the stage to their heart's content as long as he takes the money at the door. Good policy . . . '.[8]

THE DIRECTOR'S TRAINING

Shaw made few statements on how a director should be trained. He advised R. E. Golding Bright: 'When a Shakspere play is coming out – or a Sheridan one, or any old published one – buy a copy & *stage manage* [block] it yourself, marking all the business. *Then* go and see it, and you will be astonished at the grip you will have of it & how much you will learn about the stage from your mistakes & *theirs*.'[9] Customary at the first rehearsal was a reading of the play by the author (at which Shaw excelled). He advised his German translator, Siegfried Trebitsch, to practise reading the play to all of his friends until he learned how to read effectively. Later, when he read the play to the actors, he would be able to make a good initial impression.[10]

A knowledge of theatre history could be useful to the director, said Shaw, for he 'may be called on to direct a play by, say, Euripides or Aristophanes as it was produced in Athens 2,356 years ago. Or one of the pious Mysteries as the Church produced them in the Middle Ages. Or an Elizabethan drama on an Elizabethan stage. Or a Restoration or early Victorian play on a stage with proscenium, wings, and flats.'[11] His music and theatre criticism demonstrates that Shaw himself knew theatre history. In a music review, for instance, he refers to Jeremy Collier and to the concept of purity of genre.[12] One of his theatre reviews contains a reference that could only be understood in the context of Coleridge's description of Edmund Kean playing Shakespeare: 'I have no objection whatever to Satan, after elaborately disguising himself as a modern *chevalier d'industrie*, giving himself away by

[8] *Terry-Shaw*, pp. xxix, 238.
[9] Letter to R. E. Golding Bright, Sept. 26, 1896, in *Collected Letters*, p. 670.
[10] Letter to Siegfried Trebitsch, Dec. 18, 1902, Berg Collection, New York Public Library (hereafter cited as Berg Collection).
[11] *Shaw on Theatre*, pp. 287–9.
[12] *Music in London*, I, 56.

occasional flashes of lightning. Without them the audience would not know he was the devil: besides, it reminds one of Edmund Kean.'[13]

By resorting to analogy, we might glean a final Shavian prescription on the subject. If we substitute the words 'directing a play' for the words 'writing a book', we can apply to directing the precept Shaw gave to a young writer: 'If I advise you to learn to skate, you would not reply that your balance was scarcely good enough yet. A man learns to skate by staggering about and making a fool of himself. You will never write a good book until you have written some bad ones.'[14] Although analogies should never be pushed too far, it must be remembered that Shaw himself had no formal training in directing. Indeed, there was no institution where he could have acquired such training. As a director (and as a writer as well), Shaw followed his own precepts, and, having observed productions and acquainted himself with dramatic literature and theatre history, he 'learned by doing'.

THE DIRECTOR'S PREREHEARSAL PLANNING

In the Induction to *Fanny's First Play*, Count O'Dowda tells Cecil Savoyard that his daughter Fanny 'had some difficulties at the first rehearsals with the gentleman you call the producer, because he hadnt read the play . . .'. This would not have been the case with Shaw, who constantly urged careful prerehearsal planning. The elaborate stage directions in the printed texts of his plays were designed in part to make the plays more readable, but they were also meant to serve as blueprints for production.[15] 'A director cannot ignore many of [Shaw's] stage directions with impunity', Lee Simonson realized.[16] Sir Cedric Hardwicke agreed: 'Any director who attempts to stage a Shaw play without following his stage directions finds himself in trouble. They cannot be

---

13 *Our Theatres in the Nineties*, III, 18.
14 Letter to R. E. Golding Bright, Dec. 2, 1894, in Bernard Shaw, *Advice to a Young Critic*, ed. E. J. West (New York: Crown, 1955), p. 13.
15 Harris, *Bernard Shaw*, pp. 253–4; Bernard Shaw, *Plays Unpleasant*, p. xx.
16 Lee Simonson, *Part of a Lifetime* (New York: Duell, Sloan and Pearce, 1943), p. 51.

improved upon. I know, because I have tried the experiment as a director myself.'[17]

Shaw's stage directions are intended for both director and actor. 'Take the ordinary actor at a rehearsal,' he wrote to Henry Arthur Jones. 'How often does he divine without a hint from you which way your lines are to be spoken in scenes which are neither conventional nor otherwise obvious?' Shaw provided such 'hints' in his stage directions, which also aim at helping the actor to understand the character's motivation, such as 'the political or religious conditions under which . . . [he] is supposed to be acting. Definite conceptions of these are always implicit in the best plays, and are often the key to their appropriate rendering . . .'.[18] Since what is implicit is not always understood, Shaw makes these matters explicit in his stage directions.

But these stage directions are also designed for the reader. How many people, Shaw wondered, would have read Charles Dickens' novels if they had been written in the style of acting editions? He offers an example of a Dickensian novel adapted to that style: 'Sykes *lights pipe – calls dog – loads pistol with newspaper – takes bludgeon from R. above fireplace and strikes* Nancy. Nancy: Oh, Lord, Bill! (*Dies.* Sykes *wipes brow – shudders – takes hat from chair O.P. – sees ghost, not visible to audience – and exit L.U.E.*)'. If this practice is permissible for stage directions, why might it not be permissible for dialogue? Answering the question with an example, Shaw takes the first four lines of *Richard III* –

Now is the winter of our discontent
Made glorious summer by this sun of York;
And all the clouds that lour'd upon our house,
In the deep bosom of the ocean buried.

– and abbreviates them in the conventional shorthand of prose stage directions:

[17] Sir Cedric Hardwicke (as told to James Brough), *A Victorian in Orbit* (Garden City, N.Y.: Doubleday, 1961), p. 126.

[18] Letter to Herny Arthur Jones, Jan. 8, 1899, in Doris Arthur Jones, *Taking the Curtain Call: The Life and Letters of Henry Arthur Jones* (New York: Macmillan, 1930), p. 116; *Plays Unpleasant*, pp. xx–xxi.

Now is winter of our discont't
Made glorious summer by sun of York;
And all clouds th. lowered, &c.,
In deep bosom of ocean buried.[19]

Employing readable prose as a blueprint for action, his own stage directions block the movement, describe characters, provide motivations, and tell the actor what impression he should produce, though they leave the method of producing it up to him. In *Getting Married*, for instance, we find: '*Mrs Bridgenorth, her placidity quite upset, comes in with a letter; hurries past Collins; and comes between Lesbia and the General.*' Shortly thereafter, Leo '*runs in fussily, full of her own importance, and swoops on Lesbia, who is much less disposed to spoil her than Mrs Bridgenorth is. But Leo affects a special intimacy with Lesbia, as of two thinkers among the Philistines.*' These instructions not only provide the same specific blocking instructions as stage directions written in traditional abbreviations but serve other functions as well. The movement is more clearly visualized because it is given in terms not of abstract stage area (such as *XRC*) but in terms of characters ('*comes between Lesbia and the General*'). We also receive information on characterization (Leo is '*full of her own importance*'), emotional state (Mrs Bridgenorth's placidity is upset), manner of movement (Leo '*runs in fussily . . . and swoops on Lesbia*'), and character relationships (Leo and Lesbia).

In the second act of *Major Barbara* we are not told merely that '*Jenny Hill enters L, XLC – Peter Shirley on arm*', but are given a vivid and much more complete description: '*Jenny Hill, a pale, overwrought, pretty Salvation lass of 18, comes in through the yard gate, leading Peter Shirley, a half hardened, half worn-out elderly man, weak with hunger.*' This stage direction includes not only the blocking but also an account of Jenny's emotional state ('*overwrought*') and a brief character sketch of Peter Shirley that indicates the effect he should produce. Snobby Price does not merely '*XLC*'; Shaw states the manner of his movement and its motivation: '*hurrying officiously to take the old man off Jenny's*

19 *Shaw on Theatre*, pp. 92–3.

hands'. The scenery for the second act of *Major Barbara* is not described in such shorthand terms as: '*Yard. Salvation Army Shelter. January. Morning. Building U., with door C. and another door in loft above. Gateway to street L. Penthouse R., with table and benches.*' Instead, the description reads:

> *The yard of the West Ham shelter of the Salvation Army is a cold place on a January morning. The building itself, an old warehouse, is newly whitewashed. Its gabled end projects into the yard in the middle, with a door on the gound floor, and another in the loft above it without any balcony or ladder, but with a pulley rigged over it for hoisting sacks. Those who come from this central gable end into the yard have the gateway leading to the street on their left, with a stone horse-trough just beyond it, and, on the right, a penthouse shielding a table from the weather. There are forms at the table . . . .*

This stage direction gives the same information as the shorthand, but at the same time describes the appearance of the building, the weather, and the reason for scenic appurtenances. Useful to the scene designer, this information is also helpful to the actors who, in this '*cold place on a January morning*', must walk from the centre of the yard to the area shielding them from the weather, and then from the penthouse to the more open yard – their sensory responses changing as they cross.

The value of this method of writing stage directions is perhaps more apparent when one compares it with Shaw's practice *before* the first edition (1898) of *Plays: Pleasant and Unpleasant*. Prior to that edition, Shaw used precisely the type of stage direction he later deplored. The first act of the 1894 typescript of *Arms and the Man*[20] has '*Door R.2.E. with lock and key*', while the corresponding stage direction in the Standard Edition is '*The door is on the side nearest the bed*' – which is easier to visualize, for the placement of the door is described in relation to another scenic element. In 1894, '*Balcony and mountain snow backing*'; in the Standard

[20] 'Arms and the Man', 1894 typescript, Yale University Library. All further references to the 1894 version are to this typescript.

Edition, '*Through an open window with a little balcony, a peak of the Balkans, wonderfully white and beautiful in the starlit snow, seems quite close at hand, though it is really miles away*' – which is more helpful to the scene designer, for it conveys more clearly the effect to be produced. In 1894, '*Exit*'; in the Standard Edition, '*She goes out, swaggering*' – which is more helpful to the actress, for it specifically indicates the manner in which she leaves. In each case, the later version is more informative and far easier to read.

From a director's viewpoint, however, the later treatment is still incomplete. Shaw the author planned the blocking and stage business when he prepared the play for the printer. Shaw the director refined the author's blocking and stage business when he prepared the play for production.

Shaw believed that the director must plan meticulously, never leaving anything to chance that he could arrange beforehand.[21] He should prepare a prompt-book in order to save time, and come to the first rehearsals

> with the stage business thoroughly studied, and every entry, movement, rising and sitting, disposal of hat and umbrella, etc. ... settled ready for instant dictation; so that each player will be in the most effective position to deliver his lines and not have to address an intimate speech to a player at the other side of the stage, nor to follow such a player without a line or movement to transfer the attention of the audience accordingly. The exits must be carefully arranged so that the players leave the stage immediately on their last word, and not hold up the play until they have walked to the door.

Unless the director blocks the play in advance, he will waste a great deal of time during rehearsals, and unless he sets down this blocking in his prompt-book, he might, no matter how extensive his experience, forget some movements, such as exits.[22]

Before blocking the action, however, the director needs a floor plan. Shaw often sketched a plan in the margin of his prompt-book. In preparing *The Philanderer* for production, he drew

21 Letter to Siegfried Trebitsch, Dec. 10, 1902, Berg Collection.
22 *Shaw on Theatre*, pp. 280–1, 286.

such a plan above the scenic description of the second act –

> *A long room, with glass doors half-way down on both sides, leading respectively to the dining room corridor and the main staircase. At the end, in the middle, is the fireplace, surmounted by a handsome mantelpiece, with a bust of Ibsen, and decorative inscriptions of the titles of his plays. There are circular recesses at each side of the fireplace, with divan seats running round them, and windows at the top, the space between the divans and the window sills being lined with books. A long settee faces the fire. Along the back of the settee, and touching it, is a green table, littered with journals. Ibsen, looking down the room, has the dining room door on his left, and beyond it, nearly in the middle, a revolving bookcase, with an easy chair close to it. On his right, between the door and the recess, is a light library stepladder. . . .*
>
> *Cuthbertson is seated in the easy chair at the revolving bookstand, reading the Daily Graphic. Dr Paramore is on the divan in the recess on Ibsen's right, reading the British Medical Journal.* – thus:[23]

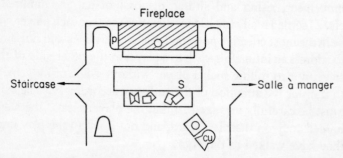

With this plan, he could more easily visualize the stage picture and the movements while blocking the action. The possibilities for varying the positions of the actors are made clearer in the floor

[23] British Museum, Add. 50597. The paperback edition used as prompt-book (London: Constable, 1906) contains no indication of a date of production, though the play was produced at the Court Theatre in 1907. The description of the set in this edition differs from the description in the Standard Edition. Unless otherwise indicated, sketches from the description in the Standard Edition. Unless otherwise indicated, sketches from Shaw's blocking notes and rehearsal notes are mine, copied from Shaw's. The specially numbered illustrations, however (Figures 1–11), are reproductions of Shaw's own drawings.

plan, which shows graphically the different stage areas created by the furniture 'breaking' the stage space.

In the margins of the prompt-script, Shaw the director blocked the action – transforming explicit movements in the text into pictorial patterns or reduced cues, elaborating and refining implicit movements, and inventing new movements that Shaw the author did not indicate. For the introduction scene at the end of the first act of *Mrs Warren's Profession,* for example, the author provided few directions. In preparing the play for production,[24] Shaw had to devise blocking that would accomplish several goals: as Reverend Samuel Gardner is introduced to the other characters, he must see and be seen by each person to whom he is introduced; Mrs Warren should have an unobstructed view of him; she should have time to observe him before crying out her recognition; and her movement should build to that recognition. As the dialogue begins, Mrs Warren and Crofts are upstage, Vivie and Frank stage-centre, Praed downstage right and Gardner downstage left. Vivie and Frank are designated by the initials of their first names, the others by the initials of their last names. Shaw blocked the scene in six movements:

	FRANK. . . . Let me introduce – my
(1) G to LC	father: Miss Warren. (1)
	Vivie (*going to the clergyman and shaking*
(2) V to C	*his hand*) (2) Very glad to see you here,
(3) F to L	Mr Gardner. (3) Let me introduce every-
(4) W down to RC	body. (4) Mr Gardner – Mr Frank
	Gardner – Mr Praed – Sir George
(5) V a step up	Crofts, and – (5) (*As the men are*
	raising their hats to one another, Vivie is
	interrupted by an exclamation from her
	mother, who swoops down on the Reverend
	Samuel).

24 British Museum, Add. 50600. The copy used was *Plays: Unpleasant* (London: Grant Richards, 1900). The prompt-book contains no indication of a date of production, though the play was first presented in London by the Stage Society at the New Lyric Club in 1902. In revising the play for the 1931 Standard Edition, Shaw rewrote this scene.

(6) W to G 　　　　Mrs Warren. (6) Why, it's Sam Gardner, gone into the church!

These movements comprise a shifting picture which begins with Mrs Warren, in a crowded centre area, almost hidden by Frank and Vivie. The centre area becomes less congested when Frank moves to stage left. Mrs Warren gradually gains more prominence: she moves toward Gardner, Vivie then clears the way for her, and finally she goes directly to centre-stage to greet him. The gradual shifts can be seen in a series of plans (only the first of which Shaw drew in the margin of his script). At the beginning of the dialogue, when Vivie asks Frank to introduce her to his father, the focus is on her and Frank; Mrs Warren is almost hidden.

　　　　　　　　W

　　　　　　　　　　　　　C

　　　　　　V　F

　　P

　　　　　　　　　　　　　　　G

When Gardner and Vivie meet each other – (1) and (2) – the focus is on them, but Vivie's movement provides Mrs Warren with space: she becomes more prominent and we can observe her.

　　　　　　　　W

　　　　　　　　　　　C

　　　　　　　F

　　　　　　　VG

　　P

After Vivie introduces herself to Gardner, Frank moves to the left (3), in sufficient time to clear the space so that his father and Crofts can see each other when they are introduced. The central area is now less crowded; Mrs Warren is set off by more space.

　　　　　　　W

　　　　　　　　　　C

　　　　　　　　　　　　　　F

　　　　　　　VG

　　　P

During these introductions, as Gardner turns from downstage right to upstage left, Mrs Warren begins to move toward him (4): she can now do so without being observed by him. Gardner first looks downstage right, at Praed.

C

W   F

VG

P

Vivie then moves upstage a step (5), giving the focus to her mother and Gardner, who is at this point looking upstage left, at Crofts.

C

F

WV

G

P

Mrs Warren steps forward to Gardner, calling his name and making him turn in a sweeping movement from upstage left to stage right.

C

F

V

WG

P

Mrs Warren has moved from upstage to stage centre as Vivie and Frank relinquish the centre area and Gardner turns more than 180 degrees to focus on her. Shaw the director has fulfilled the requirements of the scene, and the entire process occurs so quickly and smoothly that the stages are unobtrusive.

The movements in this scene derive from a basic situation in the text (one character is introduced to other characters) as well as from two explicit stage directions (Vivie going to Gardner and Mrs Warren swooping down upon him). Early in the first act, when Vivie and Praed discuss Mrs Warren, Shaw the director – in order to delineate character and help generate atmosphere – suggests movement where the stage directions indicate only that Praed rises.

PRAED rises – down to float [footlights] – back to audience.	PRAED....Of course you and your mother will get on capitally. (*He rises, and looks abroad at the view*). What a charming little place you have here! VIVIE (*unmoved*) If you think you are doing anything but confirming my worst suspicions by changing the subject like that, you must take me for a much greater fool than I hope I am.
P up to VIVIE – intimately.	PRAED. Your worst suspicions! Oh, pray dont say that. Now dont. VIVIE. Why wont my mother's life bear being talked about? PRAED. Pray think, Miss Vivie. It is natural that I should have a certain delicacy in talking to my old friend's daughter about her
(1) Away a little R from V.	behind her back.(1) You will have plenty of opportunity of talking to her about it when she comes.
(2) Up, fidgetting.	(*Anxiously*) (2) I wonder what is keeping her. VIVIE. No: she wont talk about it either. (*Rising*) However, I wont press you. (3) Only, mind this,
(3) P down again to her, protesting.	Mr Praed. I strongly suspect there will be a battle royal when my mother hears of my Chancery Lane project.
(4) P stock still.	PRAED (4) (*ruefully*) I'm afraid there will.

All of the movements in this scene are stimulated by Praed's attitude to Vivie, which is based on who she is and what she does not know. Although the text indicates urbane replies to Vivie's questions and charges, the subtext implies nervousness, for Praed fears she will learn the truth. Shaw creates movement from this subtext. As Vivie dominates the situation by remaining strongly anchored in the same stage area, Praed nervously moves about – going downstage, moving to and then away from Vivie, walking upstage as he fidgets, returning to her. The tension between text and subtext is enhanced by the movement devised by the director.

Shaw also utilized movement to underscore themes and character attitudes implicit in his dialogue. When he and Forbes Robertson jointly directed the first professional English-language production of *Caesar and Cleopatra* in 1906, Shaw carefully planned the stage business, refining to a considerable degree the directions in the printed text.[25] Here, as a final example, is a small portion of Shaw's blocking for Act I, Scene ii (the throne room of Cleopatra's palace):

Kiss.
They laugh, he with a wry face.
She takes his arm & makes him walk about with her.
L then back to C.
   C CL

CLEOPATRA. I will make all the men I love kings./ I will make you a king./ I will have many young kings, with round strong arms; and when I am tired of them I will whip them to death;/ but you shall always be my king: my nice, kind, wise, good old king.

Puts his hands on her shoulders & looks at her.
Cl recoils.

CAESAR. Oh, my wrinkles, my wrinkles! And my child's heart!/ You will be the most dangerous of all Caesar's conquests.
CLEOPATRA (*appalled*) Caesar! I forgot Caesar. (*Anxiously*) You will tell him that I am a Queen, will you not? – a

25 British Museum, Add. 50611. For the prompt-script, a paperback edition was used (London: Grant Richards, 1904).

35

| Returns – pets his arm – whispers in his ear. | real Queen./ Listen! (*stealthily coaxing him*): let us run away and hide until Caesar is gone. |

Shaw's inventive movement and business, typical of his blocking, enriches the play by creating a visual obbligato to the dialogue. It has become commonplace to say that Shaw's stage directions are so detailed that they do the director's work for him and stifle his creativity. Although these stage directions are certainly more elaborate than those of most authors, they still provide leeway enough for the imaginative director, and Shaw himself was such a director.

Among the production problems upon which Shaw exercised his imagination was the staging of crowd scenes. As a music critic he had condemned Sir Augustus Harris' production of *Les Huguenots*, comparing the staging of the crowd scenes to 'blind mans buff . . . the crowd caring for nothing but to get out of the way of the principals'; he demanded a 'stage full of people who are punctual, alert, in earnest . . .'. He had praised a production of *The Basoche*: ' . . . the movements of the crowds engaged in the action are free alike from the silly stage-drill of *opera-bouffe* and hopeless idiocy and instinctive ugliness of our Italian choristers.'[26]

As a director, Shaw gave crowd scenes the care he demanded from others, blocking the action carefully. In preparing the 1906 production of *Caesar and Cleopatra*, he wrote dialogue for the extras,[27] since it was 'the only way of getting a natural effect'.[28] In the first act, for instance, Belzanor tells the Persian that Cleopatra 'is descended from the river Nile and a black kitten of the sacred White Cat', and immediately asks, 'What then?' In the dialogue for the extras, Shaw added a response; on the cue 'the sacred White Cat', there should be a 'reverential murmur'. In composing lines that give the impression of this murmur he differentiated among the extras, one of whom becomes an

26 *Music in London*, II, 78; III, 230–1.

27 MS in the Academic Center Library, University of Texas, Austin. In my quotations from the text, I use the same edition that Shaw used in blocking the action (see above, note 25).

28 Letter to Siegfried Trebitsch, June 18, 1906, Berg Collection.

irreverent guardsman whose blasphemy starts a small argument. This conflict helps convey the impression that 'real people' rather than mere 'extras' are on stage.

Yes: the White Cat.
Yes: it is magic.
We must be careful.
I have felt that myself.
Magic.
Meaow!
Blaspheme not.
Hush-sh-sh-sh!
Silence.

When the text indicates or implies reactions from the crowds, the director specifies particular reactions. Shortly after the 'White Cat' speech, a mob tries to leave the palace. While Shaw the playwright described only the fact that there is '*An affrighted uproar in the palace*', Shaw the director worked out the '*affrighted uproar*' in detail. As the women-servants and nurses rush out of the palace in panic, their panic is individualized. Some want only to get away. Others are concerned with their material possessions: one checks packages, another asks help in carrying a bundle, another realizes she has left something behind. Each responds to the others in a different way: one looks out for a friend's safety as they descend the steps, another angrily replies to someone who has apparently bumped into her.

Be quick, be quick.
Come on: Do come on.
Have you the other bundle?
Take care of the steps.
Ayisha, Ayisha!
I am here. Come on.
Take care where youre coming, will you?
Its too heavy! help me.
I'll take the other end.
Oh, Ive forgotten the panther skin.

When in the fifth act Caesar suggests to Rufio that he become governor of Egypt, the text indicates no response from anyone but Rufio. Shaw the director, however, was concerned with the responses of all within hearing distance of Caesar's suggestion, and specified that there should be 'whispering & chattering – both soldiers & ladies'. Upon hearing Caesar's words, the Egyptian women exclaim:

> What! Rufio governor.
> That vulgar common man!
> What will Cleopatra say?
> Its a shame, so it is.
> Oh, scandalous!
> Who did he say?
> Is he actually making that great brute our governor?

The soldiers exclaim:

> Did you hear that?
> Rufio is to be a governor.
> One of us! A freedman.
> Well, why not? He is a Roman.
> Catch Cato making Rufio governor of a province.
> We are the real Republicans after all.

The women's reactions range from indignation to incredulity, the men's from delighted surprise to pride. Shaw used extras not merely to populate the stage and give the impression of a crowd, but to enrich the action by varied responses and to help build the climaxes. Nor is *Caesar and Cleopatra* an isolated instance of detailed work on crowd scenes. For the 1912 production of *Captain Brassbound's Conversion*, for example, Shaw wrote exclamations and dialogue for the five extras representing Brassbound's crew.[29]

Much of the director's preproduction planning involves such drudgery as the compilation of a property list. For the second act

---

[29] MS in the Hanley Collection, Academic Center Library, University of Texas, Austin (hereafter cited as Hanley Collection).

of *The Devil's Disciple*, Shaw went through the tedious labour of making up a detailed prop-list that included a 'big loaf' of bread (large because it is homemade), a table cover that must be cloth and also recognizably American, and a powder-horn and bullet-bag attached to the leather belt holding a pair of pistols.[30]

Whereas the properties for *The Devil's Disciple* were necessary, they were not at all unusual. When unconventional properties were required, as in *The Admirable Bashville*, Shaw gave specifications: 'A knockout sceptre for Cetewayo, not too unwieldy for a broadsword combat with Lucian's umbrella', 'Four enormous boxing gloves stuffed with feathers (eiderdown preferred)', 'A mossgrown tree trunk for Lydia to sit on, not too low, and really round, so that she can get her heels well under herself when Cashel lifts her with one finger under her chin'.[31]

Movements and motivations, business and exclamations (of the extras as well as the principals), even properties were thoughtfully planned prior to rehearsals. In order to produce the effect he wanted, to save time, and to leave as little as possible to chance, Shaw meticulously prepared every detail of production in advance of his rehearsals with the actors. Before examining Shaw's rehearsal practices, however, we must first discuss his methods of casting. The next chapter analyses both, as well as a third directorial problem, cutting the script, which may occur before or during rehearsals.

[30] MS in the Hanley Collection.
[31] Letter to Granville Barker, May 26, 1903, in *Bernard Shaw's Letters to Granville Barker*, ed. C. B. Purdom (London: Phoenix House, 1956), p. 14 (hereafter cited as *Shaw-Barker*).

III

General Directing Practices

CASTING

On January 6, 1905, Shaw suggested to Gilbert Murray that Gertrude Kingston play Helen of Troy in Murray's translation of Euripides' *The Trojan Women*. 'Of course', he added, 'I make the suggestion as a practical stage manager, comparing her, not with the ideal Helen of your imagination, but with the next best Helen you are likely to get.'[1] When Shaw cast a play, a major consideration was practicality. If Ben Webster were in the company of *John Bull's Other Island*, he considered, pondering several casting possibilities, there would then be three combinations for the roles of Larry and Keegan: '1 Webster – [William] Poel, 2 [Granville] Barker – Webster, 3 Webster – Barker.' The first, he wrote Barker, 'would set you free altogether. No. 3 would save you the trouble of learning a new part. No. 2 would save the situation if Poel proved impossible as Keegan, and Webster as Larry'. (As it turned out, Number 1 was used.) Shaw usually considered numerous possibilities and combinations. In a letter to J. E. Vedrenne, he proposed Alfred Bishop, Henry Ainley, H. B. Irving, and William Haviland as possibilities for the Bishop in *Getting Married*. 'Unless the Bishop has a touch of charm & distinction the play will fail: a stage bishop wont do. For Cecil Sykes Blakiston, Casson, Basil Gill, Lestrange, Quartermaine, Vernon Steele, Tully, Harcourt Williams, Milward are none of them right exactly; but they are not grossly impossible.'[2]

Despite his practically, however, Shaw did not lose sight of the

---

1 'Bernard Shaw to Gilbert Murray', *Drama*, n.s., XLII (Autumn 1956), 27.
2 Letters: to Granville Barker, July 29, 1906, in *Shaw-Barker*, p. 66; to J. E. Vedrenne, April 6, 1908, Hanley Collection.

necessity of placing the right actor in the right role. After advising James Welsh, an actor-director who planned to produce *You Never Can Tell*, that he would be better as the Waiter than as Phil, Shaw warned him that although the play as a whole is 'absolutely actor proof', it has a ten-minute episode 'during which it is the most difficult comedy in the Irish language': the scene between Valentine and Gloria at the end of Act II. 'If that scene fails, the play fails. And nobody but a comedian of the very first forty-pound-a-week order can touch that scene. It is not that a lesser man can only do it badly: it is that *he cant do it at all.* . . . Can you get Hawtrey, or Wyndham, or John Drew, or Bourchier?'[3] To Lawrence Langner, of the Theatre Guild, Shaw suggested several doubling combinations for *Back to Methuselah*. The same actor could play Adam, Conrad, the Accountant General, and the Envoy; the same actress, Eve, Mrs Lutestring, the Oracle, and the She-Ancient. Caine, Burge, Burge-Lubin, Napoleon, and Ozymandias could be played by the same actor, and Savvy, Zoo, and the Newly Born by the same actress.[4]

In attempting to persuade actors to undertake certain roles, Shaw used charm, wit, and blarney. On March 30, 1894, he tried to interest Alma Murray in playing Raina in *Arms and the Man*:

I want Miss [Florence] Farr to play, *not* the heroine, but the servant. If I can persuade her to to this, and to crown her magnanimity by allowing you to play the heroine, will you consent to be approached on the subject, or have you any decisive objection or prior engagement that puts you out of the question? The lady does not swear, nor does she throttle the servant like the heroine in my other play [*Widowers' Houses*]. She has to make herself a little ridiculous (unconsciously) once or twice; but for the most part she has to be romantically beautiful or else amusing in a bearably dignified way. She is a

---

3 Letter to James Welsh, Jan. 30, 1899, Berg Collection. Welsh did play the Waiter, as Shaw suggested. Valentine was not played by any of the actors Shaw suggested but by Yorke Stephens.

4 Lawrence Langner, *G. B. S. and the Lunatic* (New York: Atheneum, 1963), p. 42.

Bulgarian, and can, I suppose, wear extraordinary things if she wishes.[5]

In an effort to convince Louis Calvert that he should play Undershaft in *Major Barbara*, he described the role as 'Broadbent and Keegan rolled into one, with Mephistopheles thrown in' and prophesied that Calvert's performance as Undershaft would immediately thrust Henry Irving and Beerbohm Tree into the third rank of their profession. 'There are the makings of ten Hamlets and six Othellos in his mere leavings,' wrote Shaw. 'Learning it will half kill you; but you can retire the next day as pre-eminent and unapproachable.' Since the character must play the trombone, the playwright added, Calvert would receive a fringe benefit: '. . . trombone players never get cholera nor consumption – never die, in fact, until extreme old age makes them incapable of working the slide.'[6]

In selecting a cast, Shaw believed, the director should not be concerned with whether the actors understand the play, but whether their ages, physical appearances, and personalities are suitable.[7] Refusing to offer Lillah McCarthy the role of Ellie Dunn in *Heartbreak House*, he explained to her that Ellie must be 'born to immaculate virginity', and asked, 'How can you, at your age and with your reputation as a Siddonian "heavy", play an ingenue of eighteen against two women of forty playing off their sexual fascinations for all they are worth? You could do it perfectly well [as Margaret Knox in *Fanny's First Play*] against Mrs Gilbey and Mrs Knox, but not against Hesione and Ariadne.'[8]

The peculiar 'quality' of an actor was another important consideration. Shaw complained that Elizabeth Robins projected

[5] Letter to Alma Murray, March 30, 1894, in *Letters from George Bernard Shaw to Miss Alma Murray (Mrs Alfred Forman)* (Edinburgh: Printed for Private Circulation, 1927), Letter VIII (no pagination). Shaw was successful: Alma Murray played Raina and Florence Farr played Louka.

[6] Letter to Louis Calvert, July 23, 1905, in *Shaw on Theatre*, p. 107. Calvert played Undershaft in the first production of *Major Barbara*. Broadbent and Keegan are characters in *John Bull's Other Island;* Calvert had played the former role.

[7] *Shaw on Theatre*, p. 280.

[8] Letter to Lillah McCarthy, undated, in Lillah McCarthy, *Myself and My Friends* (New York: Dutton, 1933), pp. 204-5.

youthful individualism in revolt too strongly to play successfully the role of Ella Rentheim in *John Gabriel Borkman*.[9]
Charles Charrington, he said, completely failed as Helmer in *A
Doll's House*, not through any fault of his own but because the
role was uncongenial to his natural 'quality': 'What is wanted for
Helmer is complacency *without* conviction. Charrington has
conviction without complacency . . . . It is a case of congenital
incapacity . . . '. To Granville Barker, he explained the difficulty of
casting Snobby Price in *Major Barbara*:

> Unless I can get Cremlin and Yorke [as Peter Shirley and Bill
> Walker] fitted with the right sort of Snobby we shall get the
> usual stock-company ensemble with no character at all in it.
> Of course [Edmund] Gwen can play a thief. He can also play
> the emperor of China. An actor is an actor and a part is only a
> part when all's said. . . . I want a slim, *louche*, servant-girl-biga-
> mist, half-handsome sort of rascal, *not* a costermonger, *not* an
> Artful Dodger, not anything like Gwenn.[10]

The *Lumpenproletariat* Snobby Price is an unlikeable scoundrel,
not an ingenious, colourful cutpurse. Shaw may have feared that
Gwenn, unable to eradicate his own charm and warmth, would
turn Snobby into a likeable scoundrel, appealing to the audience
in a way that Snobby should not appeal, and, in effect, justifying
the character. As Shaw said in another context, 'Making [wicked
characters] lovable is the most complete defence of their conduct
that could possibly be made'.[11]

Shaw frequently referred to the roles in his plays in terms of
stock-company types: Judith Anderson (*The Devil's Disciple*)
should be played as a melodramatic heroine, Lady Britomart
(*Major Barbara*) as a *grand dame*.[12] He also referred to these roles
in operatic terms. In casting plays, he said, the director should pay

9 *Our Theatres in the Nineties*, III, 126–7.
10 Letters: to Janet Achurch, April 21, 1892, in Shaw, *Collected Letters*, p. 337; to
Granville Barker, Sept. 28, 1905, in *Shaw-Barker*, p. 53. Arthur Laceby played Snobby.
11 *Shaw on Theatre*, p. 2.
12 Letters: to William Faversham, April 19, 1917, Hanley Collection; to Theresa
Helburn, 1928 (no month or day cited), in Langner, *G.B.S.*, pp. 109–10.

attention to vocal contrast. 'The four principals should be soprano, alto, tenor, and bass'.[13] In *Arms and the Man*, Raina and Louka should be soprano and contralto, respectively. Bluntschli's voice should be dry, and Sergius' ringing.[14]

Shaw was aware, too, of the importance of securing believable family relationships. For example, it is easy to cast the roles in *You Never Can Tell* separately, but difficult when the family is taken into account, for the actors must be convincing not only as the characters but as parents, children, sisters, and brother of each other. Mrs Clandon and Dolly should be believable as mother and daughter, Gloria and Dolly as sisters.[15]

CONDUCTING REHEARSALS

At the start of rehearsals, Shaw believed, the author should read the play to the company. If the author was not a competent reader, a substitute should do the job. If a good substitute were unavailable, however, it would be better to have no reading at all, rather than a bad one.[16] Shaw himself usually read the play to the cast. From this first reading, Sir Cedric Hardwicke recalls, the actors learned 'how the author wished the various parts to be acted. . . . The inflexions of voice peculiar to each character were steadily maintained until the end. . . . Shaw's soft Irish tones never became monotonous, nor even in the most dramatic moments did he resort to gesture; he merely relied on the modulations of his voice to make his meaning clear.' Once this reading was over, 'It was difficult for any of us to go seriously astray, knowing now precisely what the author had in mind'.[17]

Ideally, Shaw would like to have 'a half dozen rehearsals seated round a table, books in hand, to get *the music* right before going on to the stage'. Since these conditions did not exist in the

13 *Shaw on Theatre*, p. 280.
14 Letter to Cecil Lewis, April 18, 1932, Berg Collection.
15 Letter to Yorke Stephens, May 21, 1900, Enthoven Collection, Victoria and Albert Museum, London (hereafter cited as Enthoven Collection).
16 *Shaw on Theatre*, p. 280.
17 Cedric Hardwicke, *Let's Pretend: Recollections and Reflections of a Lucky Actor* (London: Grayson and Grayson, 1932), pp. 201–2; Hardwicke, *A Victorian in Orbit*, p. 155.

British theatre, he did his best 'to get, not what I want, but what is possible under the circumstances'.[18] Because of this, blocking began immediately. 'If the scenery is not ready,' he told Siegfried Trebitsch, remarking that in England it is never ready,

> I seize chairs, forms &c. with my own hands, and arrange them to mark doors and objects of furniture. (The stage manager waits until he can order a carpenter to do it, as such manual work would compromise his dignity.) I open the promptbook; seize the actor or actress who begins; lead them to their entrance in my pleasantest and busiest and friendliest manner, and say, 'Here you are: this is your entrance – now down here and across to there' letting them read the words just as they please, and simply piloting them through the movements.

After blocking the first act, he asked the actors to run through the act again in order to settle the movements and business in their memories. The two run-throughs took up one rehearsal. The following day he would run through the second act twice in the same manner, and the next day the third.[19] At this point, according to Shaw, the director should be on the stage with the actors, prompting them as they go through the business. They should be asked not to learn their roles until after the first week of rehearsals (the blocking rehearsals), for 'nothing is a greater nuisance than an actor who is trying to remember his lines when he should be settling his position and getting the hang of the play with his book in his hand'. Once the blocking had been completed and the movements mastered, the director should ask the actors whether they were comfortable in these movements, and if not, which movements were uncomfortable. He should then adjust the movements so that the actors can perform them comfortably.[20]

At the end of this first stage of rehearsals, Shaw would have the director call '[line] perfect' rehearsals. As the actors go through

18 Letter to Mrs Patrick Campbell, Jan. 29, 1920, in *Bernard Shaw and Mrs Patrick Campbell: Their Correspondence*, ed. Alan Dent (New York: Knopf, 1952), pp. 232–3 (hereafter cited as *Shaw-Campbell*).
19 Letter to Siegfried Trebitsch, Dec. 18, 1902, Berg Collection; *Shaw on Theatre*, p. 155.
20 *Shaw on Theatre*, pp. 156, 281.

the scenes without scripts in hand, the director should leave the stage and sit in the auditorium. During this phase of rehearsals, he must not stop the scene and demand that the actors repeat a passage again and again until they get it right. This, Shaw believed, is schoolmastering rather than directing. Such repetitions cause the performance of that passage to deteriorate rather than to improve. If anything goes wrong, or if the director thinks of an improvement, let him make a note, and give this note to the actor at the end of the act. But he should not mention or attempt to correct a fault until its repetition reveals that the actor will not correct it in his own way as he is learning the play. When '[line] perfect' rehearsals begin, Shaw reminds the director, there will be at least a week of disappointing and agonizing backsliding, for as the actor tries to memorize his lines, everything else will be lost. At this stage, the director should be especially considerate of the actor, for he is under a heavy strain. Only the inexperienced director will betray dismay at this stage of rehearsal, and permit himself outbursts of reproach or frenzied attempts to make sure that everything is perfect at every rehearsal.

Once the memorizing stage has been passed, says Shaw, the director must watch the act run-throughs and take careful notes, appending 'Rehearse this' after some of them. At the end of the act, he should have the actors go through those bits to get them right. Still, he must refrain from schoolmastering, that is, ordering them to repeat a scene even if it means staying there all night. During this phase, he may return to the stage, interrupting as often as he finds necessary. Shaw implies that this should not occur often, and ideally not at all.[21]

'Remember that no stranger should be present at a rehearsal', Shaw advised. Since he recognized that it was sometimes expedient for strangers – such as newspapermen – to attend, he suggested a prearranged interruption to remind the visitors that they were witnessing a rehearsal rather than a performance. This interruption should consist of an instruction to a member of the technical staff about a technical detail. The director should never

[21] *Ibid.*, pp. 156–8, 281–3; letter to Siegfried Trebitsch, Dec. 18, 1902, Berg Collection.

direct an actor in the presence of strangers, and he should always get the consent of every actor before admitting a stranger to rehearsal.[22] According to Sir Cedric Hardwicke, Shaw practised what he preached: 'Rehearsals to Shaw were as confidential as the confessional.' If a stranger were present, 'Shaw punctiliously abstained from giving a single word of instruction to any actor until the auditorium was clear again'. Hardwicke called this an 'infallible instinct for good theatrical etiquette'.[23]

Consideration for the actor is also evidenced in Shaw's advice on scheduling rehearsals. First, the director should not waste the actor's time. Actors with only a few lines should not wait all day while the principals rehearse. Second, he should avoid late-night rehearsals. If he cannot, then he should see that the actors receive taxi fare home if they are kept until the last trains and buses have stopped.[24]

'Never find fault until you know the remedy,' Shaw urged the director. If something is wrong and the director does not know how to correct it, he should say nothing, for it is discouraging for an actor merely to be told that something is wrong. The director should be silent until a solution comes to him – or to the actor, as it probably will. Since the actor cannot assimilate more than two or three suggestions at a time, the director should remember not to give him too many notes at one rehearsal. If he thus controls his zeal and saves the other notes for future rehearsals, the actor may correct some of the errors by himself. Further, the director should not discuss such trifles as mistakes in lines or business as if the fate of the world hinged on them. Nor should he discuss anything that is not essential. And he should be prepared for the actor to make the same mistake several times in succession, and to forget his directions until they have been given, also in succession, for several days.[25]

If an actor 'repeatedly omits some physical feat or movement, the director must conclude that it is made impossible by some

22 *Shaw on Theatre*, p. 159.
23 Hardwicke, *A Victorian in Orbit*, pp. 127–8.
24 *Shaw on Theatre*, p. 284.
25 *Ibid.*, pp. 156–7, 283; letter to Siegfried Trebitsch, Dec. 18, 1902, Berg Collection.

infirmity which the player would rather die than disclose. In such cases the business must be altered.' The director should not discuss a passage with the actor, nor should he tell him that a scene is essentially either pathetic or comic. If he does, 'the player will come to the next rehearsal bathed in tears from the first word to the last, or clowning for all he is worth all the time'. Instead, he should demonstrate to the actor – not as an order, but as a suggestion – how the passage or scene should be performed. These demonstrations should be so exaggerated that there is no chance of the actor merely imitating them. 'A performance in which the players are all mimicking the director instead of following his suggestions in their own different ways, is a bad performance.'[26]

Imitative performances, Shaw knew, followed the law of doing what was done the last time, whereas living, organic performances obeyed the innermost impulse of the text. 'And as that impulse is never, in a fertile artistic nature, the impulse to do what was done last time, the two laws are incompatible, being virtually laws respectively of death and life in art.' Shaw recalls having laughed at a provincial Iago who, at the words, 'Trifles light as air', twitched his handkerchief into space. A theatrical acquaintance rebuked him, claiming that the actor was right because he had copied every gesture, movement, and inflection of his performance from Charles Kean. 'Unfortunately', Shaw points out, 'he was not Charles Kean: consequently Charles Kean's [by-] play no more fitted him than Charles Kean's clothes. . . . In the old provincial stock companies . . . there was often to be found an old lady who played Lady Macbeth when the star Shakespearean actor came his usual round. She played it exactly as Mrs Siddons played it, with the important difference that, as she was not Mrs Siddons, the way which was right for Mrs Siddons was the wrong way for her.' While this was written in 1889,[27] before Shaw had any directing experience, the principles

26 *Shaw on Theatre*, pp. 283, 287.
27 Bernard Shaw, *How to Become a Musical Critic*, ed. Dan H. Laurence (New York: Hill and Wang, 1961), pp. 260, 262.

of 'death and life in art' apply to Shaw's directing. He wanted the actor to use his own methods, to follow his own impulses, rather than to imitate Shaw's or anyone else's techniques. 'There is only one effect to be produced,' he pointed out, 'but there may be fifty different ways of producing it'; and 'a good part can be played a dozen different ways by a dozen different actors and be none the worse: no author worth his salt attaches a definite and invariable physiognomy to each variety of human character. Every actor must be allowed to apply his own methods to his own playing.'[28]

Shaw followed these precepts. 'Dont hamper your inspiration,' he urged Annie Russell, who was rehearsing the title role of *Major Barbara*. 'If I make suggestions or offer criticisms freely it is only on the understanding that you need not give them a second thought if they do not chime in with your own feeling.' Reluctant to suggest a method of playing the final scene with Cusins because he did not know exactly how she got her effects ('except that it is not in my rhetorical, public-speaker kind of way'), he implored her to play the role in her way rather than in his: 'You have much greater resources in the direction of gentleness than I have; and I assure you you will go wrong every time you try to do what *I* like instead of letting yourself do what *you* like.'[29]

One must remember that in this instance Shaw was dealing with an accomplished actress, not a novice. To a novice, his advice was different. He told Molly Tompkins not to take the bit between her teeth all at once, but to take a night for herself, or an act, or – as a beginning – a speech or two, and test whether her method proved to be as good as the coached method. The only way to win a conflict with the director, he asserted, was to make her method convincing. Possibly, her method was right but she did not yet have the skill to put it across. If this were the case, then for the moment she must accept the coaching. Nevertheless, 'in the end you must make yourself something more than a marionette

28 Letter to Louis Wilkinson, Dec. 6, 1909, in Harris, *Bernard Shaw*, p. 254; Bernard Shaw, *Pen Portraits and Reviews*, p. 276.

29 Letters to Annie Russell, Nov. 20 and 27, 1905, Manuscript Room, New York Public Library.

worked mostly by somebody who is not a successful actor or author or critic or connoisseur or anything else that commands an unquestioning deference'.[30]

The director should not get angry and complain in the pedantic manner of a schoolmaster that he has repeatedly called attention to such and such a point, for he 'will destroy the whole atmosphere in which art breathes, and make a scene which is not in the play, and a very disagreeable and invariably unsuccessful scene at that'.[31] Nor should he shame the actor by calling out his deficiencies before the entire company. Shaw's practice was to give quiet, individual advice to the actors after each run-through.[32]

Numerous actors praised Shaw's good manners, his tact, and his ability to communicate his ideas.[33] According to the Frank Harris biography (and the passage may have been written by Shaw himself, who corrected the galleys after Harris died),[34] 'Shaw's manners were always ingratiating, his directions always helpful, and altogether he carried an air of angelic sweetness while he sometimes undid the work of weeks of another man quite as competent as himself in the matter at issue. His manners alone saved him from being hit with an axe.' The only instance I have found of Shaw's having lost his temper was when Mrs Patrick Cambell's violent refusal to execute a mechanical movement provoked him into calling her an amateur.[35]

Shaw understood that there are different types of actors, each of whom must be treated differently. The director 'must dis-

[30] *To A Young Actress: The Letters of Bernard Shaw to Molly Tompkins,* ed. Peter Tompkins (New York: Potter, 1960), p. 41 (hereafter cited as *Shaw-Tompkins*).

[31] *Shaw on Theatre,* p. 157.

[32] G. W. Bishop, *Barry Jackson and the London Theatre* (London: Barker, 1933), p. 27.

[33] For example: Forbes Robertson (Sir Johnston Forbes-Robertson, *A Player Under Three Reigns* [Boston: Little, Brown, 1925], p. 129), Lillah McCarthy (McCarthy, *Myself and My Friends,* p. 59), Sir Cedric Hardwicke (Hardwicke, *Let's Pretend,* p. 203), Dame Sybil Thorndike and Sir Lewis Casson (Mander and Mitchenson, *Theatrical Companion to Shaw,* pp. 13–4, 17).

[34] Harris, *Bernard Shaw,* p. 419. Shaw is quoted as having called the book 'My autobiography by Frank Harris' (Hesketh Pearson, *G. B. S.: A Postscript* [New York: Harper, 1950], p. 7) and having said, '*I* wrote the book' (Allan Chappelow [ed.], *Shaw the Villager and Human Being* [London: Skilton, 1961], pp. 150–1). The passage quoted in the text is in Harris, *Bernard Shaw,* p. 247.

[35] Draft of letter to Edith Craig, July 17, 1940, Burgunder Collection.

tinguish between born actors who should be let alone to find
their own way, and spook actors who have to be coached
sentence by sentence and are helpless without such coaching.
There are so many degrees between these extremes that the tact
and judgment of directors in their very delicate relations with
players are sometimes strained to the utmost. . . .'[36]

He often tried to ease the strain by clowning. 'What Raina
wants', he wrote Lillah McCarthy after a rehearsal, 'is the
extremity of style – style *Comédie Française*, Queen of Spain
style. Do you hear, worthless wretch that you are? STYLE.'
He demanded that Mrs Patrick Campbell, as Eliza in *Pygmalion*,
not run to Higgins like her pet dog, and then 'forget everything in
an affectionate tête à tête with him. Imagine that he is the author,
and be scornful.'[37] The day after the first performance of *Major
Barbara* he wrote Louis Calvert, who had failed to learn all his
lines,

> I see with disgust that the papers all say that your Under-
> shaft was a magnificent piece of acting, and Major Barbara a
> rottenly undramatic play, instead of pointing out that Major B
> is a masterpiece and that you are the most infamous amateur
> that ever disgraced the boards.
>
> Do let me put [Cremlin] into it. A man who could let the seven
> deadly sins go for nothing could sit on a hat without making
> an audience laugh. I have taken a box for Friday and had a
> hundredweight of cabbages, dead cats, eggs, and gingerbeer
> bottles stacked in it. Every word you fluff, every speech you
> unact, I will shy something at you. Before you go on the stage
> I will insult you until your temper gets the better of your liver.
> You are an imposter, a sluggard, a blockhead, a shirk, a
> a malingerer, and the worst actor that ever lived or that ever
> will live. I will apologize to the public for engaging you. I will
> tell your mother of you. Barbara played you off the stage;
> Cremlin dwarfed you; Bill annihilated you; Clare Greet took

36 *Shaw on Theatre*, p. 285.
37 Letters: to Lillah McCarthy, undated, in McCarthy, *Myself and My Friends*,
p. 94; to Mrs Patrick Campbell, April 11, 1914, in *Shaw-Campbell*, p. 180.

all eyes from you. If you are too lazy to study the lines I'll coach you in them. That last act MUST be saved or I'll withdraw the play and cut you off without a shilling.[38]

Shaw's extravagant manner may have softened his criticism, but it did not conceal that criticism, nor did it hide the unmistakable urgency of his effort to make Calvert learn his lines.

Shaw's clowning sometimes took the form of parody. Writing to Alma Murray that her performance in *Arms and the Man* lacked 'the sincerity of the noble attitude and the thrilling voice', he exaggerated that attitude in his complaint: 'What – oh what has become of my Raina? How could you have the heart to lacerate every fibre in my being? . . . Oh, that first act! that horrible first act! could anything expiate it? I swear I will never go to the theatre again. Here is my heart, stuck full of swords by your cruel hands.' Beneath a drawing of a heart with nine swords in it, the letter is signed, 'Yours, agonised'. A few weeks later his tone was considerably different as he apologized to his leading lady:

> I have now to entirely withdraw all my former observations, which you will please attribute to temporary aberration. It is quite impossible that you could ever have played Raina otherwise than beautifully. . . . I shall not now accept your invitation to call and talk the part over, because whenever any woman gives me the pleasure your playing tonight did, I

[38] Letter to Louis Calvert, Nov. 29, 1905, in *Shaw on Theatre*, pp. 109–10. Cremlin's name, when it appears in brackets, is indicated by a dash in *Shaw on Theatre*. The name is given in the text of the letter printed under 'George Bernard Shaw as a Man of Letters: The Correspondence with Which He Enlivened the Beginnings of "Major Barbara"', *The New York Times*, Dec. 5, 1915, Sec. VI, p. 6. Among the Annie Russell papers in the Manuscript Division of the New York Public Library is a typed copy of this letter, which Louis Calvert probably made or had made (it is typed on the reverse side of a play booking form headed 'Mr Louis Calvert's Companies') at Miss Russell's request. Differing from the published versions in several, chiefly minor, details, its major variation (for our purposes) is that in place of the reference to 'Barbara' it refers to 'Barker'. Whether this copy is more or less accurate than the published versions is not known.

Calvert's mother, Mrs Charles Calvert, was a famous actress. F. Cremlin played Peter Shirley in the 1905 production and apparently understudied Undershaft; Clare Greet played Rummy Mitchens. The statement that Clare Greet took all eyes from Calvert may refer to the end of the second act, wherein Undershaft 'buys' the Salvation Army. Rummy Mitchens is at that point sitting in the loft, doing and saying very little.

cannot help falling violently in love with her; and I can no longer support the spectacle of Forman's [her husband's] domestic happiness. He is a most intolerable usurper and monopolist; and the advantage he has taken of the mere accident of his knowing you before I did appears to me to be altogether unjustifiable.

In case she might think he was in such good humour that his appreciation was worthless, he added some adverse criticism before signing the letter, 'Yours contritely'.[39] In this instance, the actress herself resolved the errors that prompted Shaw's tirade. When Wendy Hiller was rehearsing *Saint Joan* at Malvern in 1936, Shaw wrote her a letter containing devastating criticisms of her acting. She called at his hotel to discuss the points raised in his letter. 'He was charming & courteous,' she reports, 'but not inclined to take me or his notes too seriously – I was overcome with earnestness which I think he found amusing.'[40]

Shaw did not on all occasions use a charming manner to soothe ruffled feelings. When the occasion called for it, he was frank. To Lillah McCarthy, for example, he wrote, 'Raina has gone to bits . . . the effect is disastrous.' He then gave reasons. But on other occasions, he would offer praise, telling the same actress that her Ann Whitefield (*Man and Superman*) 'was one of the best performances I have seen you do'.[41] His praise was valued partly because it was not given indiscriminately. In his discussions with and letters to actors, he did not withhold praise. He used it sincerely, but also as a way to reassure the actor that his performance was not 'all wrong'. This obvious device – honoured as often in the breach as in the observance – was nonetheless effective. Shaw made special use of it in the 'pep-talks' (or 'pep-letters') he gave to actors shortly before opening night. After offering several pieces of adverse criticism on Lillah McCarthy's

39 Letters to Alma Murray, May 11, 1894, and June 1, 1894, in *Letters from George Bernard Shaw to Miss Alma Murray*, Letters X and XI.
40 Letter, Wendy Hiller to author, July 12, 1964.
41 Letters to Lillah McCarthy, undated and June 7, 1905, in McCarthy, *Myself and My Friends*, pp. 70, 93.

Raina, he called them 'only counsels of perfections', reassuring her that 'even if you miss a few points, you have enough in hand for a handsome success'. He used the same tactic with John L. Shine, who played Larry Doyle to Louis Calvert's Broadbent in *John Bull's Other Island*. This time he called the adverse criticisms 'danger signals', and went on to say, 'Even if we make a slip or two, there is enough in hand now for success. . . . On the whole, whatever happens to the play, you will score.' But his pre-opening-night letters did not always contain such praise. His letter to Mrs Patrick Campbell, headed 'FINAL ORDERS', written just before the opening of *Pygmalion*, contains no praise, but a series of instructions and an admonition to leave as little as possible to chance.[42]

Prior to opening night, however, is the final stage of preparation, dress rehearsal. During this stage – when the actor must accustom himself to performing in costume, under lights, using full properties and scenery – the director should be prepared for everything to go wrong. This should not deter him: after the run-throughs he should return to the stage – with his notes – to rehearse the sections that need polishing. Shaw believed the theatrical superstition that a bad final rehearsal meant a good performance, since the actors would otherwise be too confident to achieve success on opening night.[43]

The time needed to direct a play, Shaw estimated, was four weeks: one week for blocking the action; two weeks for memorizing, with the director seated in the house, taking notes; and a week for dress rehearsal.[44] He apparently adapted these methods to traditional rehearsal practices in England, for he also stated that ideally he would like a rehearsal period of from six weeks to two months.[45]

CUTTING AND CHANGING THE SCRIPT

Shaw issued numerous critical strictures against cutting and chang-

[42] Letters: to Lillah McCarthy, undated, in *ibid.*, p. 92; to John L. Shine, Oct. 29, 1904, Hanley Collection; to Mrs Patrick Campbell, April 11, 1914, in *Shaw-Campbell*, pp. 179–81.

[43] *Shaw on Theatre*, pp. 282–3.

[44] *Ibid.*, p. 283.

[45] Letter to Mrs Patrick Campbell, Jan. 29, 1920, in *Shaw-Campbell*, pp. 232–3.

ing Shakespeare's plays. 'In a true republic of art', he declared in a review of the Lyceum *Cymbeline*, 'Sir Henry Irving would ere this have expiated his acting versions on the scaffold. He does not merely cut plays: he disembowels them. In Cymbeline he has quite surpassed himself by extirpating the antiphonal third verse of the famous dirge. A man who would do that would do any-thing – cut the coda out of the first movement of Beethoven's Ninth Symphony, or shorten one of Velasquez's Philips into a kitcat to make it fit over his drawing room mantlepiece.'[46] Irving, he predicted, 'will have an extremely unpleasant quarter of an hour if he is unlucky enough to come across the Bard in the heavenly Pantheon'.[47] But Irving was not the only villain. Shaw chastised John Barrymore for having cut an hour and a half of the text of *Hamlet*, including the recorder scene, the scene with with the King after Polonius' death, and the speech beginning 'How all occasions do inform against me'. And Augustin Daly's rearrangement of the scenes in *Two Gentlemen of Verona*, he claimed, made the plot and the character relationships unin-telligible.[48]

In 1887, in a review of Richard Wagner's *On Conducting*, he approvingly quoted Wagner's charge that cutting is the con-ductors' 'means of accommodating to their own incompetence the artistic tasks which they find impossible'. In 1919 he made the same charge against producers who cut Shakespeare:

The moment you admit that the producer's business is to improve Shakespear by cutting out everything that he himself would not have written, and everything that he thinks the audience will either not like or not understand, and every-thing that does not make prosaic sense, you are launched on a slope on which there is no stopping until you reach the abyss where Irving's Lear lies forgotten. The reason stares us in the face. The producer's disapprovals, and consequently his cuts,

46 *Our Theatres in the Nineties*, II, 197–8.
47 *Shaw on Theatre*, p. 104. The statement is from 'The Dying Tongue of Great Elizabeth', reprinted from the *Saturday Review*, Feb. 11, 1905. Irving died on Oct. 14, 1905.
48 *Shaw on Theatre*, pp. 167–8; *Our Theatres in the Nineties*, I, 170–1.

are the symptoms of the differences between Shakespear and himself; and his assumption that all these differences of superiority on his part and inferiority on Shakespear's, must end in the cutting down or raising up of Shakespear to his level.

According to Shaw, the only workable plan is to perform Shakespeare's plays in their entirety. This plan makes Shakespeare, not the director, the ultimate authority. If the latter thinks Shakespeare's language is half-dead and often unintelligible, these are excellent reasons for not producing the plays, but poor reasons for 'breaking them up and trying to jerry-build modern plays with them, as the Romans broke up the Coliseum to build hovels'. Those people who really want to see Shakespeare want all of him, and not merely a director's 'favorite bits; and this is not in the least because they enjoy every word of it, but because they want to be sure of hearing the words they do enjoy, and because the effect of the judiciously selected passages, not to mention injudiciously selected passages, is not the same as that of the whole play. . .'. Cutting, Shaw concludes, 'must be dogmatically ruled out'. Either perform a Shakespearean play in its entirety or else leave it alone. 'If Shakespear made a mess of it, it is not likely that Smith or Robinson will succeed where he failed.'[49]

Shaw praised William Poel's productions of Shakespeare *in toto* and applauded Forbes Robertson for breaking with stage tradition by including Reynaldo and Fortinbras in his production of *Hamlet*. In Shaw's short story *The Theatre of the Future* (1905), a Utopian theatre performs the three parts of *Henry VI* plus *Richard III* on four different evenings, without altering or revising the texts, since the management 'has, unfortunately, not succeeded in obtaining the services of a stage manager whose judgment in these matters can be accepted as unquestionably superior to Shakespear's'.[50]

[49] Shaw, *How to Become a Musical Critic*, p. 131; *Shaw on Theatre*, pp. 122–6.
[50] *Our Theatres in the Nineties*, III, 202; Bernard Shaw, *The Black Girl in Search of God and some lesser tales*, p. 151.

But what of Shaw's own judgement in this regard? At times, he himself was willing to cut Shakespeare. In 1896, he offered Ellen Terry advice on cutting and rearranging the dialogue of *Cymbeline*, and in 1937 he rewrote the last act, calling his version *Cymbeline Refinished*. It was 'idiotic', he told Ellen Terry on the former occasion, to retain such 'tawdry trash' as

> No, 'tis slander,
> Whose edge is sharper than the sword, whose tongue
> Outvenoms all the worms of Nile. . . .

> (III, iv, 35-37)

He suggested that Imogen not read aloud Posthumus' letter to her (III, iv, 21-31) but instead have Pisanio read it aloud in Act III, Scene ii, so that the first sentence of the letter would motivate his 'How! of adultery?' (line 1), and the remainder provoke his 'How! that I should murder her?' (line 11). Then, in the fourth scene, Imogen would read the letter in silence and exclaim, 'I false!' – thus moving the words from line 48 to before line 32. Pisanio would reply, 'What shall I need to draw my sword? The paper / Hath cut her throat already. What cheer, madam?' – cutting Shakespeare's eight lines to two. Imogen's entire speech beginning 'Thou didst accuse him of incontinency' (lines 49–59) should be deleted, Shaw urged, together with the 'rubbish' about 'false Aeneas' (lines 60-66).[51]

This advice seems to contradict Shaw's condemnation of those who cut Shakespeare's texts. However, because he knew that Irving would cut the play, his letter might also be regarded – in part, at any rate – as an effort to secure an intelligent cutting. Supporting this suggestion is a statement in Shaw's preface to *Cymbeline Refinished*: 'I shall not press my version on managers producing Cymbeline if they have the courage and good sense to present the original word-for-word as Shakespear left it, and the means to do justice to the masque. But if they are half-hearted about it, and inclined to compromise by leaving out the

---

51 Letters to Ellen Terry, Sept. 6 and 8, 1896, in *Terry-Shaw*, pp. 41–2.

masque and the comic jailor and mutilating the rest, as their manner is, I unhesitatingly recommend my version.'

About his own plays he unhesitatingly insisted upon his version.[52] He ordered Siegfried Trebitsch to tell the people at the Volkstheater of his absolute refusal to have a line deleted or a comma changed. 'If they know how plays should be written, let them write plays for themselves. If they dont, they had better leave the business to those who do.' And if they are too backward to be capable of performing his plays as he wrote them, 'they can let them alone. . . '. 'If you find at rehearsal that any of the lines [in *Candida*] cannot be made to go', he wrote Richard Mansfield, 'sack the whole company at once and get in others. I have tested every line of it in my readings of the play; and there is a way of making every bit of it worth doing.' According to Shaw, by cutting *Misalliance*, William Faversham caused the play's failure and made himself useful only as an example of an actor-manager who succeeded when he followed Shaw's instructions and failed when he did not.[53]

Actually, it was not cutting that Shaw objected to, but bad cutting. 'I dont mind cuts,' he said, 'but I'll make them myself so that the point of my sermons is not destroyed.'[54] In his 'Rules for Play Producers', he admitted, 'A play may need to be cut, added to, or otherwise altered, sometimes to improve it as a play, sometimes to overcome mechanical difficulty on the stage, sometimes by a passage proving too much for an otherwise indispensable player.'[55] But cutting to save time never 'works', for it usually saves time at the expense of the play.[56] Intelligent cutting, however, is a skilled job which 'should be done by the author, if available, or if not, by a qualified playwright. not by a player, nor the callboy'.[57]

[52] Mander and Mitchenson, *Theatrical Companion to Shaw*, p. 6.

[53] Letters: to Siegfried Trebitsch, June 26, 1902, in Henderson, *George Bernard Shaw*, pp. 482–3; to Richard Mansfield, March 16, 1895, in *Collected Letters*, p. 499; to William Faversham, Dec. 9, 1917, Hanley Collection.

[54] Hardwicke, *A Victorian in Orbit*, p. 253.

[55] *Shaw on Theatre*, pp. 284–5.

[56] Letter to J. B. Fagan, Oct. 20, 1921, Burgunder Collection.

[57] *Shaw on Theatre*, p. 285.

When Max Reinhardt agreed to direct *Ceasar and Cleopatra* for Berlin's Deutsches Theater, Shaw suggested that in order to bring the performances into the traditional time limits, Reinhardt cut Act III (the lighthouse act). Reinhardt did not follow this advice, but instead cut the burning of the library at the end of Act II and also the first scene of Act IV. Shaw was furious: 'May the soul of Reinhardt scream through all eternity in burning brimstone!' he wrote Granville Barker, and wondered how the second act could possibly be intelligible without the burning of the library.[58] It is always a mistake, he explained, to trust people like Reinhardt to alter a play: 'They see the effects, but they dont see the preparation of the effects – the gradual leading of the audience up to them. They cut the preparation out, and then are surprised because the effects misfire.' Reinhardt, he concluded, 'has done everything that a thoroughfaced blockhead could do to achieve a failure; and he has achieved it accordingly . . . . May his soul perish for it!'[59]

Although Shaw refused to sanction other people cutting and changing his plays, he often did so himself.[60] On some occasions, he made cuts only for specific productions, later restoring the passages – sometimes with minor modifications – to the printed texts. Shaw removed part of the following passage, for example, from the 1905 production of *Major Barbara* (brackets indicate deletions):

---

[58] *How to Become a Musical Critic*, p. 253; letter to Granville Barker, May 7, 1906, in *Shaw-Barker*, p. 62.

[59] Letter to Siegfried Trebitsch, May 7, 1906, Berg Collection.

[60] For instance, he cut Mrs Higgins' speech about the Eynsford Hills from the third act of *Pygmalion*: 'What a horrible thing poverty is! That poor woman was brought up in a rich country house; and she cant understand why her children, without any education or any chances, dont get asked anywhere. Why will people living in a grove off the Fulham Road with a general servant and a hundred and fifty pounds a year call themselves the Eynsford Hills and go on as if they had five thousand'. Although Shaw gave no reason for removing the passage, he may have felt that it was too explicit. The passage appears in Shaw's 'rehearsal edition' of the play: *Pygmalion: A Play in Five Acts: by a Fellow of the Royal Society of Literature* (London: Constable, 1913), University of North Carolina Library. All later references to the rehearsal edition of *Pygmalion* are to this copy. For information on Shaw's use of special rehearsal editions, see F. E. Loewenstein, *The Rehearsal Copies of Bernard Shaw's Plays* (London: Reinhardt and Evans, 1950).

BARBARA. . . . But you came and shewed me that I was in the power of Bodger and Undershaft. [Today I feel – oh, how can I put it into words? Sarah: do you remember the earthquake at Cannes, when we were little children? – how little the surprise of the first shock mattered compared to the dread and horror of the second? That is how I feel in this place today.] I stood on the rock I thought eternal; and without a word of warning it reeled and crumbled under me. I was safe with an infinite wisdom watching me – an army marching to Salvation with me; and in a moment, at a wave of your cheque book, I stood alone; and the heavens were empty. [That was the first shock of the earthquake: I am waiting for the second.] [61]

While he provided no explanation for the deletions, the cut passage is essentially digressive. Without Barbara's reminiscence her speech is more straightforward, compact, and vigorous. In the Standard Edition, Shaw restored the passage and changed 'at a wave of your cheque book' to the more accurate 'at a stroke of your pen in a cheque book'. Shortly after this speech he cut part of another passage:

UNDERSHAFT. . . . Only fools fear crime: we all fear poverty. Pah! (*He turns on Barbara*) [You talk of your half saved ruffian in West Ham: you accuse me of dragging his soul back to perdition. Well, bring him to me here; and I will drag his soul back again to salvation for you. Not by words and dreams; but by thirtyeight shillings a week, a sound house in a handsome street, and a permanent job. In three weeks he will have a fancy waistcoat; in three months a tall hat and a chapel sitting; before the end of the year he will shake hands with a duchess at a Primrose League meeting, and join the Conservative Party.
BARBARA. And will he be the better for that?
UNDERSHAFT. You know he will. Dont be a hypocrite, Barbara. He will be better fed, better housed, better clothed, better behaved; and his children will be pounds heavier and bigger. That will be better than an American cloth mattress in a

[61] Typed prompt-script, 'Major Barbara', Houghton Library, Harvard College.

shelter, chopping firewood, eating bread and treacle, and being forced to kneel down from time to time to thank heaven for it – knee drill, I think you call it.] It is cheap work converting starving men with a Bible in one hand and a slice of bread in the other . . . .

Here, too, Shaw restored the passage to the printed edition. Again, he gave no reason for the cut. A reasonable speculation, however, is prompted by Shaw's letter to Calvert after the play's opening night (above, pages 51–2): since Calvert had difficulty memorizing the lines, Shaw may have cut some long speeches to enable him to devote his time to other, more important passages.

For the 1921 production of *Heartbreak House*, Shaw cut sixty-five lines from the third act (1919 edition), all of which he retained in subsequent editions of the play. For these cuts, however, he provided a reason: the actors were unable to deliver these lines convincingly. 'There are always lines which are dud lines with a given cast,' he explained to J. B. Fagan, his co-director of the 1921 production. 'Change the cast and you get other lines dud. The line which strikes on A's box will only bother B.'[62]

The different versions of Shaw's plays demonstrate that he made numerous changes in the dialogue and stage business. In the second Act of *Arms and the Man,* the 1894 typescript copy contains this exchange between Petkoff and Catherine:

PET- The war's over. The treaty was signed three days ago at Bucharest; and the decree for our army to demobilize was issued yesterday. It's an honorable treaty: it declares peace but not friendly relations: the two words have been expressly struck out. If the Austrians hadnt interfered we'd have annexed Servia and made Prince Alexander Emperor of the Balkans. Confound them!

CATH- (*Sitting R. of table*) Well, never mind, dear. So glad to have you back again with me.

62 Letter to J. B. Fagan, Oct. 20, 1921, Burgunder Collection.

PET-   Thank you, my love. I missed you greatly!
CATH-   (*Affectionately*) Ah! (*Stretches her hand across the table to squeeze his.*)

In the Standard Edition, this was changed to:

PETKOFF.... The war's over. The treaty was signed three days ago at Bucharest; and the decree for our army to demobilize was issued yesterday.

CATHERINE (*springing erect, with flashing eyes*) Paul: have you let the Austrians force you to make peace?

PETKOFF (*submissively*) My dear: they didnt consult me. What could *I* do? (*She sits down and turns away from him*). But of course we saw to it that the treaty was an honorable one. It declares peace –

CATHERINE (*outraged*) Peace!

PETKOFF (*appeasing her*) – but not friendly relations: remember that. They wanted to put that in; but I insisted on its being struck out. What more could I do?

CATHERINE. You could have annexed Serbia and made Prince Alexander Emperor of the Balkans. Thats what I would have done.

PETKOFF. I dont doubt it in the least, my dear. But I should have had to subdue the whole Austrian Empire first; and that would have kept me too long away from you. I missed you greatly.

CATHERINE (*relenting*) Ah! (*She stretches her hand affectionately across the table to squeeze his.*)

The later version, partially the result of several productions of the play, is richer. When Petkoff informs Catherine of the demobilization order, the later version has her responding violently, forcing him to explain that he was unable to prevent the action. In the earlier version, his declaration that the treaty was honourable and declares peace merely follows the information about the demobilization. In the later version, it is an attempt to pacify Catherine, who has first accused him and then turned away from him. Far from pacified, Catherine is outraged, interrupts him again (as she does not do in the earlier version), and forces him to deliver the remainder of his speech as a further effort to appease her. In the earlier version, Petkoff pompously announces the desirability of annexing Serbia and making Prince Alexander a Balkan Emperor. In the later version, Shaw transfers this speech from the romantic husband to the ferocious wife, deleting her uncharacteristically conciliatory dismissal of the proposed annexation. Petkoff then – in the later version – gives a romantic explanation of his inaction which functions as a transition to wooing his wife. Her acquiescence is a gradual development in the newer version. In 1894, Catherine's jingoism, firmly established in the first act, disappears from this second-act scene. She is not angry at the peace; she ignores it, telling Petkoff that she is glad he has returned. When he confesses that he missed her, she cries, '(*Affectionately*) Ah!' and reaches across the table to squeeze his hand. In the new version, she is angry and he is conciliatory. Only after his flattering explanation that a prolongation of hostilities would have kept him from her for too long, does she change. When he confesses that he missed her, she is still not immediately affectionate but cries, '(*relenting*) Ah!' and *then* reaches '*affectionately*' across the table to squeeze his hand. The new version is more polished; uncharacteristic lines are cut or changed and new lines added to reveal more clearly the characters' attitudes and relationships with other characters.

Shaw frequently incorporated into his printed texts changes made during rehearsals. On August 20, 1897, he wrote Edith Craig – who had played Prossy in *Candida* – that he was preparing an edition of his plays (*Plays: Pleasant and Unpleasant*):

> Will you send me a line to remind me of the business in the scene with Eugene at the place where you say 'Pray are you flattering me or flattering yourself'. Do you go back to the typewriter at the end of that speech or at 'I'll leave the room, Mr M[arch]b[anks]: I really will. It's not proper'. I want to get it right for the printer.

Also, if you have accumulated any effective gags, you might let me have them for inclusion in the volume.[63]

Although there is no record that he did include any gags that Edith Craig accumulated, the printed edition shows that she starts to return to the typewriter at the first speech, that Marchbanks stops her, and that she resumes her seat at the typewriter after the second speech.

Another example of Shaw's practice of revising the printed text to include business that was added during rehearsals is the following series of changes he made in the first act of *Arms and the Man*. In the 1894 typescript, Raina gives Bluntschli the box of chocolates. He eats the contents and says, 'Creams! Delicious!' Shaw expanded this for the first edition of *Plays Pleasant* (1898). After the exclamation, Bluntschli *'looks anxiously to see whether there are any more. There are none. He accepts the inevitable with pathetic goodhumor. . . '*. During rehearsals for the 1919 revival, Shaw suggested to Bluntschli that after he has gobbled the contents of the box, 'Search for another & lick your fingers'.[64] This note was incorporated into the Standard Edition (1931), where the earlier stage-direction has been enlarged to read: *'He looks anxiously to see whether there are any more. There are none: he can only scrape the box with his fingers and suck them. When that nourishment is exhausted he accepts the inevitable with pathetic goodhumor. . . '*.

Pygmalion offers a further example of the printed text incorporating rehearsal changes. In the 1913 rehearsal edition, the action of the third act begins:

The door is opened violently; and Higgins enters.
MRS HIGGINS (*dismayed*) Henry! What are you doing here today? It is my at-home day: you promised not to come.

During rehearsals of the 1914 London production, Shaw wrote a note for Higgins and Mrs Higgins: 'Hat biz.'[65] In the Standard Edition the 'Hat biz' is spelled out for future directors: *'Higgins*

63 Letter to Edith Craig, Aug. 20, 1897, *Collected Letters*, p. 797.
64 Rehearsal notes, *Arms and the Man*, 1919, Burgunder Collection.
65 Rehearsal notes, *Pygmalion*, 1914, Hanley Collection.

enters with his hat on.' Following Mrs Higgins' line is the business: '*As he bends down to kiss her, she takes his hat off, and presents it to him.*' Exclaiming, 'Oh brother!' Higgins then '*throws the hat down on the table*'.

Shaw frequently cut and changed his plays – to shorten the running time, to assist an actor who could not adequately deliver the lines, to improve the play. On some occasions, Shaw restored cut passages to the printed editions of his plays. We may conclude that in such cases the deletions were made because of the requirements of a particular production. At other times, changes (often extensive) were incorporated in printed editions of the play. All changes and cuts, Shaw insisted, were the prerogatives of the author, who understood the relationship of each line to the total fabric of the play. Rather than entrust the cutting of his plays to an unskilled vivisector – however capable a director or actor he might be – Shaw preferred that his plays be produced in their entirety.

IV

The Actor

THE ACTOR'S AIMS

According to Shaw, the actor's function, like the director's, is 'to make the audience imagine for the moment that real things are happening to real people'.[1] Shakespeare, according to Shaw, had a similar idea when he made Hamlet declare that 'it is the business of the players to make their highly artificial declamation seem to be natural human speech. One can almost hear him say to Burbage at rehearsal, "Speak as if you were a human being, Dick, and mean something by what you are saying. Dont rant" '.[2] The actor's job 'is not to supply an idea with a sounding board, but with a credible, simple, and natural human being to utter it when its time comes and not before'.[3] Nor is it his task to make a play pleasing or interesting, for that is the author's business. He advised the young actress Molly Tompkins not to confuse

> the appreciation and understanding of parts and plays with the ability to act them. If the two were the same faculty then Shakespear would have been a greater actor than Burbage, and I should be able to play Cleopatra better than you. An actor stands in much the same relation to an author as a carpenter or mason to an architect: he need not understand the entire design in the least; and he would not do his part of the job any better for such understanding.[4]

In creating a credible human being, moreover, the actor should display no sign of effort. The title character of Shaw's novel

---

[1] Bernard Shaw, *Pen Portraits and Reviews*, p. 266.
[2] Undated inscription in *The Tragedie of Hamlet*, ed. J. Dover Wilson, ill. Edward Gordon Craig (Weimar: Cranach Press, 1930), Hanley Collection.
[3] *Our Theatres in the Nineties*, III, 128.
[4] Letter to Molly Tompkins, July 16, 1922, in *Shaw-Tomkins*, pp. 23-4.

66

Cashel Byron's Profession probably speaks for the author when he says, 'If a thing cant be done light and easy, steady and certain, let it not be done at all. . . . The more effort you make, the less effect you produce . . . in all professions any work that shews signs of labor, straining, yearning . . . or effort of any kind, is work beyond the man's strength that does it, and therefore not well done.' As Cashel Byron observes, 'the same is true in other arts'.[5] The actor who displays physical strain not only fails to produce the effects for which he strives, he also makes his audience acutely uncomfortable. To play his role without physical strain, he must have training.

THE ACTOR'S TRAINING

On June 12, 1927, *The New York Times* printed a letter from Shaw to Alexander Bakshy, in which he admitted that Bakshy was right

> in saying that my plays require a special technique of acting, and, in particular, great virtuosity in sudden transitions of mood that seem to the ordinary actor to be transitions from one 'line' of character to another. But, after all, this is only fully accomplished acting; for there is no other sort of acting except bad acting, acting that is the indulgence of imagination instead of the exercise of skill.[6]

'The exercise of skill' is a frequent theme in Shaw's writings on the actor. Deriding unskilled actors who spend their time 'idly nursing their ambitions, and dreaming of "conceptions" which they could not execute if they were put to the proof', he maintained that the 'conceptions' of the unskilled 'are mere impertinences'.[7] The art of acting is 'impossible without tremendous practice and constant aiming at beauty of execution, not through a mechanical study of poses and pronunciations (though every actor should be a plastic and phonetic expert), but through a

---

5 *Cashel Byron's Profession*, pp. 91-2.
6 *Shaw on Theatre*, p. 185.
7 *Our Theatre in the Nineties*, II, 127-8, 191.

cultivation of delicate feeling, and absolute renunciation of all the coarser elements of popularity'.[8] Training is essential.

> The defect of the old-fashioned systems of training for the stage was that they attempted to prescribe the conclusions of this constantly evolving artistic sense instead of cultivating it and leaving the artist to its guidance. Thus they taught you an old-fashioned stage-walk, an old-fashioned stage-voice, an old-fashioned stage way of kneeling, of sitting down, of shaking hands, of picking up a handkerchief, and so on, each of them supposed to be the final and perfect way of doing it. The end of that was, of course, to discredit training altogether. But neglect of training very quickly discredits itself. . . .[9]

Cannot an actor acquire the necessary training in the process of performing first smaller and then larger roles? Although a public speaker might learn his profession at the expense of his audience, Shaw did not believe that an actor could do so, for 'a public speaker practises his whole art every time he speaks, whereas an inexperienced actor applies only a small portion of his art to such minor parts as he is likely to obtain at first. Repeating that minor part every night for six months will not advance him as a skilled actor. . . .' Suppose a young man is cast as Paris in *Romeo and Juliet*. Since, in all likelihood, he is unable to dance a minuet or to fence, he will have to be coached in these arts. Just as the repetition of a minuet for 150 performances will not make him a fully qualified dancer, neither will his repetition of the role of Paris make him a fully qualified actor.[10] 'A fully qualified actor', according to Shaw, is one who 'can perform and sustain certain physical feats of deportment, and build up vocal climaxes with his voice through a long crescendo of rhetoric'. He also has a 'feeling for splendor of language and rhythm of verse'.[11] He 'knows the visible symptoms of every human condition, and has such

[8] Letter to Charles Charrington, March 1, 1895, in *Collected Letters*, p. 492.

[9] *Our Theatres in the Nineties*, I, 212.

[10] Bernard Shaw, 'Qualifications of the Complete Actor,' *Dramatic Review*, Sept. 19, 1885, British Museum, Add. 50691.

[11] *Pen Portraits and Reviews*, p. 274.

perfect command of his motor powers that he can reproduce with his own person all the movements which constitute such symptoms'. Conceding that this 'ideal standard of perfection has not yet been realized', Shaw nevertheless maintains that 'it is necessary to determine the standard in order to keep ... actors ... from going astray'.[12]

Since this ideal standard, admittedly unattained, may also be unattainable, cannot the actor rely on inspiration to prevent him from going astray? Although Shaw valued the role of inspiration in art ('I depend entirely on inspiration,' he once said,[13] using an exaggerative adverb), he also valued hard work (he researched the American Revolution, for example, in preparation for *The Devil's Disciple*).[14] More important, perhaps, he understood their relationship: groundwork should be so thorough that if inspiration does not arrive, the job will still be done adequately. When Ellen Terry worried that her performance as Imogen in *Cymbeline* would misfire, Shaw reminded her that she had prepared the role thoroughly and pointed out that if she played for all she were worth, she could not 'fall below a good weekday performance, even if [she were] not in the vein for a regular Sunday one'.[15] In order 'to make effective and visible *all* [his] artistic potentialities', the actor must study and master all of the technical devices of his profession. 'In my own art', he affirmed, 'I am ready, if only time be given me, to answer for the workmanship to the last comma; and now, if "inspiration" comes, it does not half escape me: I know how to seize it and knead it so as to exhaust all the nutriment in it.' He would have the actor do the same, developing his physical, intellectual, and emotional resources to the point that he is capable of seizing, kneading, and exhausting the nutriment of any inspiration that may come to him.[16] If the inspiration does not arrive,

12 'Qualifications of the Complete Actor'.
13 Henderson, *George Bernard Shaw*, p. 748.
14 Handwritten notes on back of printed ticket to British Museum Reading Room, Texas; *Three Plays for Puritans*, pp. 76–82.
15 Letter to Ellen Terry, Sept. 21, 1896, in *Terry-Shaw*, p. 59.
16 Letter to Florence Farr, May 1, 1891, in Florence Farr, Bernard Shaw, and W. B. Yeats, *Letters*, ed. Clifford Bax (New York: Dodd, Mead, 1942), pp. 2-3.

these resources should be sufficiently developed to enable him to give the 'good weekday performance' he mentioned to Ellen Terry.

Physical training is essential, for the actor must have full command of his motor powers. As a music critic, Shaw called attention to operatic performers who failed to train their bodies. He mocked some of the singers at early Bayreuth performances of Wagner as 'animated beer casks, too lazy and conceited to practise the self-control that is expected as a matter of course from an acrobat, a jockey or a pugilist'. As a drama critic, he advised gymnastic training to enable the actor to control all parts of his body.[17] As a director, he gave the same advice. Lillah McCarthy relates that when Shaw noticed that she acted with her muscles contracted, he had her learn muscular control. After a month of such lessons, 'I could move any muscle and relax it as I wished, and from this time my acting developed a greater naturalness. I learned to move more easily and, when standing still, to remain if need be quite immobile.'[18]

The actor's voice, as well as his body, should be trained, so that he can communicate intelligibly without shouting. Shaw, who strongly emphasized voice and articulation, had considerable knowledge of these skills. The voice teacher George John Vandeleur Lee had moved into the Shaw household when Bernard was eleven, and singing became part of his upbringing. Beyond learning the Lee method of voice production, he worked on a revision of Lee's 1869 book *The Voice: Its Artistic Production, Development, and Preservation*.[19] And, of course, Shaw also reviewed concerts and operas for many years, and wrote a book on Wagner.

Shaw advised diaphragmatic breathing, together with a steady, economical, unforced expulsion of air, rather than a voice-cracking 'tension of [vocal] cords and force of blast',[20] for the latter produced 'a muscular strain . . . that . . . destroyed the voice,

---

[17] Bernard Shaw, *Major Critical Essays*, p. 273; 'Qualifications of the Complete Actor'.
[18] McCarthy, *Myself and My Friends*, p. 68.
[19] *London Music*, p. 18; Rosset, *Shaw of Dublin*, pp. 116-21, 203-4. A typed manuscript, dated 1882 and entitled 'The Voice', is in the Berg Collection.
[20] *Music in London*, II, 157-8; *London Music*, p. 158.

and sometimes killed the vocalist'.[21] Because tension and force could destroy the speaking as well as the singing voice, Shaw cautioned Molly Tompkins, 'Do not ... imagine that the vigorous speech that is needed for public purposes is shouting because at first it seems more violent than ordinary conversation. Real shouting is no use: it does not travel. . . . As far as mere loudness goes, never go to the utmost of your power: always keep well inside it. It is articulation that tells.' He also condemned the exaggerated force achieved by what is called glottal shock, which is the 'sudden and energetic drawing together of the lips of the glottis an instant before expiration commences'. In less technical terms, he explained: 'I myself, in the very rare instances when I pronounce the word "I" in a self-assertive mood, may sometimes attack it with a *coup de glotte*; but I always regret it the moment the sound strikes my conscience, which, in my case, as in that of all musical critics, is situated in my ear.'[22] Not only does the glottal shock offend the ear of the sensitive hearer, its habitual use would offend the voice of the speaker or singer.

Deprecating the 'artificial woolly boom'[23] that results from using the throat to obtain resonance, Shaw urged the speaker and singer to develop all resonating chambers. He would have each individual learn his own optimum pitch. In a review of J. P. Sandlands' *How to Develop General Vocal Power*, he repudiated the author's advice that all students should learn to speak at the pitch of 'F in the bass', which Sandlands identified as 'the foundation tone'. The reverse is true, said Shaw, for the 'so-called "foundation tones" vary with each individual . . .'. The consequence of attempting to use 'F in the bass' as a foundation tone, when one's voice is too high, is apt to be 'clergyman's sore throat', which is 'brought on by persisting in what Artemus Ward calls "a sollum vois" '.[24] Unless the voice employs its widest range,

21 'The Voice', p. 26.

22 Letter to Molly Tompkins, Dec. 10, 1922, in *Shaw-Tompkins*, p. 29; *Music in London*, II, 248.

23 Copy of letter to Charles Charrington, April 15, 1900, British Museum, Add. 50532.

24 The review appeared on Nov. 12, 1886, British Museum, Add. 50692. The file does not contain the name of the periodical.

strain develops. Censuring both Verdi and Sir Arthur Sullivan for allowing the singer to use only a part of his vocal range, Shaw praised Handel and Wagner for 'employing the entire range of the human voice,' which helped to relieve any particular vocal register from fatigue and also exercised all registers.[25] With a full knowledge of the necessity for vocal variety, he disparagingly defined both Yeats's 'cantilation' and Bernhardt's *voix d'or* as 'intoning'. He compared the latter to 'holding down one key of an accordian. . . . Some critics speak of "the melody" of it, as to which I can only say that the man who finds melody in one sustained note would find exquisite curves in a packing case'.[26]

Shaw demanded good diction. Ellen Terry, whose articulation he particularly admired, 'had her professional technique hammered into her in her childhood by Mrs Charles Kean, who would sit in the gallery and see to it that every word of Ellen's reached her there'.[27] To develop what Shaw called an 'athletic articulation', the actor must be drilled in a 'staccato alphabet so staccatissimo that every consonant will put out a candle at the back of the gallery. Not until [his] tongue and lips are like a pianist's fingers should [he] begin to dare think of speaking to an audience.' 'Alphabet' meant chiefly 'consonants', for Shaw agreed with 'the old rule': '. . . take care of the consonants and the vowels will take care of themselves.'[28] For purposes of public speaking, he himself 'practised the alphabet as a singer practises scales until I was in no danger of saying "Loheeryelentheethisharpointed sword" instead of "Lo, *I l*end *th*ee *th*iss *sh*arp *p*ointed sword" '.[29] To Janet Achurch he suggested alphabet exercises:

> To practise R (trilled), repeat L. M. N. R: this will, if you leave your tongue loose, bring it into the right position. Then try, first eer, ér, èr &c, and ree[,] ré, rè &c; and then such combinations as BRee, bré, brè &c, and eebr, ébr, èbr &c,

25 *Music in London*, III, 44-5, 60; *Major Critical Essays*, p. 275.
26 Farr *et al.*, *Letters*, pp. 21-2; *Our Theatres in the Nineties*, I, 162.
27 *Terry-Shaw*, pp. xi, xxxiv.
28 Farr *et al.*, *Letters*, p. 22; *Shaw-Campbell*, pp. 305-6.
29 Bernard Shaw, *Sixteen Self Sketches*, p. 64.

proceeding with CR, DR, FR, GR, PR, SR, TR. The terminal RD is very important; and then there is RF (serf) RP (harp) RT (art) &c. Also of course, such combinations as SP, TH, BL, CL, DL, FL, GL, PL, SL, TL, & so on, compiling them out of the alphabet in order.[30]

Shaw was familiar with exercises for vowels as well as for consonants. In his revision of Lee's technical manual on the voice, for instance, he set down exercises designed to prevent vowels from becoming diphthongs: '. . . if the a in ray ends as ee, it is a diphthong, and the student must persevere until the sound of the French é can be sustained as long as the breath lasts, the tip of the tongue never once rising to the front teeth after the articulation of the initial r. . .'.[31] In a scene written for the film version of *Pygmalion*, he composed a diction lesson on the same subject:

HIGGINS. . . . Say A, B, C, D.

LIZA (*almost in tears*) But I'm sayin it. Ahyee Bǝyee, Cǝ-yee –

HIGGINS. Stop. Say a cup of tea.

LIZA. A cappǝtǝ-ee.

HIGGINS. Put your tongue forward until it squeezes against the top of your lower teeth. Now say cup.

LIZA. C-c-c – I cant. C-Cup.

PICKERING. Good. Splendid, Miss Doolittle.

HIGGINS. By Jupiter, she's done it at the first shot.[32]

Since the language of poetry is not colloquial, poetry involves special problems of articulation:

. . . you must take great care of the words that are not used in ordinary conversation, because the audience cannot guess them and will not take the meaning in so quickly as when you are giving them common idiomatic phrases. If you say

Woff terangelsthrough thisguise, Fa rabove yonazh erplane you might as well say it in Chinese. You must say Waftt hher,

30 Letter to Janet Achurch, Jan. 29, 1896, in *Collected Letters*, p. 592.

31 Farr *et al.*, *Letters*, p. 22; 'The Voice', p. 9.

32 Standard Edition, p. 242. The upside-down e is the phonetic symbol of the 'schwa vowel', or the 'obscure vowel', pronounced as the second vowel in *other*.

no matter how pedantic it sounds. But it wont sound pedantic to the audience. . . .

Vowels, though, should not be distorted. *Angels* should not rhyme with *bluebells* or *organ* with *dustpan*. The second vowel of each, 'the Obscure Vowel', must rhyme with the second vowel in *butter*.

Still, vocal technique was to Shaw not an end but a means and should therefore be unnoticed by the audience. 'Practise all this until it becomes completely automatic,' he advised the novice actor, 'for there is nothing more annoying than an actress or a singer who is thinking about her technique when she ought to be thinking only of the sense and feeling of her part.'[33] All of the technical skills which the actor so painstakingly acquires should be concealed, and the actor's behaviour on stage appear so spontaneous and inevitable that it would be impossible to persuade the audience that any art or study is involved. Finally, there is the old saw – nonetheless true – that to be a complete actor one must be a complete human being. In an interview, the pianist Madame Backer-Gröndahl told Shaw (as Corno di Bassetto) 'that it is as wife and mother that she gets the experience that makes her an artist'. He responded, 'I collapse. Bassetto is silenced. He can only bow to the eternal truth, and think how different his column would be if all artists were like this one.'[34]

Although the acting skills that have been discussed can be taught in a classroom or rehearsal room, an academy aiming to train actors should not confine its instructional programme to the class- or rehearsal room, for part of the actor's necessary training includes appearing before audiences. As analogy Shaw uses the medical profession. Just as the apprentice doctor must 'walk the hospitals as well as . . . pass examinations' in order to receive his degree, so should the apprentice actor 'walk the stage for a couple of years before receiving a diploma as master of what can be taught in his art'. Unless an acting academy includes this period of internship for the trainee, the graduates of this institution will earn their livelihoods only 'by teaching others to win the same

[33] Letter to Molly Tompkins, Dec. 10, 1922, in *Shaw-Tompkins*, p. 30.
[34] *Our Theatres in the Nineties*, I, 212; *London Music*, p. 163.

degree for the same purpose', and thereby leave the art of acting 'to be practised by people without degrees, who, when they are conspicuously successful can be made honorary graduates, and thus throw a radiance on the institution which can never proceed from within itself'.[35]

Shaw knew that the conditions which he postulated as desirable did not exist. In his novel *Love Among the Artists* which describes some of the conditions that did exist, he gives the case history of the development of an actress, who studies elocution and learns her craft by performing in provincial stock-companies before coming to London.[36] Far from upholding the provincial stock-company as a training ground for actors, Shaw deplored it, calling the notion that stock-companies taught versatility 'the wildest of delusions. Versatility was the much needed quality of which [stock-company actors] became quite incapable.' With weekly or nightly programme changes, actors 'have to "swallow" their speeches as best they can, and deliver them, not in the author's characterization, but in their specialities such as juvenile lead, ingénue, walking gentleman, light comedian, low comedian, singing chambermaid (soubrette), heavy old man (*père noble*), old woman, utility, and so forth'. The most that he could say for the stock-company was that it taught the actor 'the routine of his business'. The routine items included 'conscientiously articulated elocution which reached the back row of the pit effectively (it is really more satisfactory to hear an actor say meechee-yah-eeld and know that he means my child than to hear him say msha and wonder what on earth the fellow thinks he is mumbling)', a 'pompous entrance which invited and seized the attention of the audience', and a 'momentous exit on the last word of his last speech (your modern novice as often as not finishes in the middle of the stage and stops the play until the audience has enjoyed the spectacle of his walking to the door)'. This 'routine of his business', however, was satisfactory only for routine acting. With

---

35 'Proposed Diploma in Dramatic Art', carbon-copy, dated June 25, 1922, Hanley Collection.
36 Bernard Shaw, *Love Among the Artists*, pp. 101-2, 113-25.

such abilities an actor could 'completely . . . kill the dramatic illusion of a modern play'.[37]

In 1886, Shaw invited the theatregoer nostalgic for the 'palmy days' to study palminess at the opera, which still operated on the basis of the theatrical stock-company. There, such abuses of the stock-company system as the substitution of mannerisms for acting, the use of the same stage caricature for each role, and the insufficiency of rehearsal would make it obvious that 'the palmy theory lacks experimental verification'. Shaw preferred the long-run system, for the actor who knows one role thoroughly 'is superior to the actor who can scramble with assistance [from a prompter] through a dozen. The one gets into the skin of one character: the other puts on the clothes of twelve.'[38]

But the long-run system, too, has its curses, for it engenders mechanical repetition and saps vitality. Reviewing the 789th performance of *Dorothy*, Shaw asserted that the tenor, 'evidently counting the days until death should release him from the part of Wilder', sang 'as if with the last rally of an energy decayed and a willing spirit crushed'. Similarly, a lacklustre languor character-ized the ninety-fifth of the one hundred performances of Forbes Robertson's production of *Hamlet*, whose actors 'were for the most part sleep-walking in a sort of dazed blank-verse dream. Mr Barnes raved of some New England maiden named Affection Poo', Mrs Patrick Campbell's 'subtle distinctions . . . between madness and sanity had blurred off into a placid idiocy turned to favor and to prettiness', and Forbes Robertson's 'lightness of heart [was] all gone . . .'. This deterioration was the result of 'the torturing fatigue and monotony of nightly repetition', which drove the actor 'to limit himself to such effects as he can repeat to infinity without committing suicide'.[39]

Admitting that 'the playing-every-night system is only possible for *routine* acting',[40] Shaw still found it superior to the

37 Bernard Shaw, *The Matter with Ireland*, ed. David H. Grene and Dan H. Laurence (London: Hart-Davis, 1962), p. 12; *Shaw on Theatre*, p. 286; *Terry-Shaw*, p. xxi.
38 *How to Become a Musical Critic*, pp. 113-6.
39 *London Music*, p. 214; *Our Theatres in the Nineties*, III, 270-1.
40 Letter to Ellen Terry, July 4, 1897, in *Terry-Shaw*, p. 184.

stock-company system, for 'the modern actor may at all events exhaust the possibilities of his part before it exhausts him, whereas the stock actor, having barely time to apply his bag of tricks to his daily task, never varies his treatment by a hair's breadth from one half century to another'. To avoid the debilitating effects of the long-run system without returning to the old stock-company system, some actors and actresses had a repertory of plays that provided resting places: Charles Surface, for instance, relieved Richard III, Mirandolina relieved Magda. While an improvement on both the stock-company and the long-run systems, this method was more of a mitigation than a solution, for 'no actor can possibly play leading parts of the first order six nights a week all the year round unless he underplays them, or routines them mechanically in the old stock manner, or faces a terrible risk of disablement by paralysis, or, finally, resorts to alcohol or morphia. . . '. Shaw's answer to the problem was a repertory company with alternate casts: Sir Henry Irving and Ellen Terry, for example, playing *Hamlet* on Thursdays and Saturdays, Forbes Robertson and Mrs Patrick Campbell playing it on Wednesdays and Fridays. On the other two nights, all four would appear in a comedy.[41] To put it in more general terms: Shaw would have a repertory company with a sufficient number of major performers that the burden on any one of them would not be too heavy.

DEGREES OF REALISM

As a director wanting his actors to convince the audience that real things were happening to real people, Shaw demanded illusionistic acting. He noted that on the French stage, a kiss was 'as obvious a convention as the thrust under the arm by which Macduff runs Macbeth through'. It was 'purposely unconvincing', designed to make it impossible for anyone to believe that it was real. On the English stage, by contrast, realism was carried to the point at which only the actors were aware that the kiss was not real. Shaw favoured the English method, for whatever question

[41] *Our Theatres in the Nineties*, III, 272-3.

may arise as to the propriety of representing an incident on the stage, he found it offensive, once it was decided to represent that incident, to do it other than convincingly.[42]

Shaw's directorial practices followed the English tradition. During rehearsals of *You Never Can Tell*, he demanded that the company behave 'as if they were coming into a real room instead of . . . rushing to the float [footlights] to pick up the band at the beginning of a comic song'.[43] Charles Charrington's activities in the Fabian Society, Shaw suggested, might be spoiling his acting: 'You are getting rhetorical; and you expound and illustrate your parts like the Ghost in Hamlet.'[44] Shaw's rehearsal notes contain many similar injunctions, as the following examples illustrate. When Louka tells Sergius that Bluntschli is worth ten of him, she should merely refer to Bluntschli rather than make an obvious stage-cross. Liza's interruption of Higgins' departure, 'Before you go, sir', should not be rendered melodramatically as 'Before you go, Serrrrrr', but instead should be spoken naturally. When Higgins equates Liza's offer of a shilling for English lessons with a millionaire's sixty to seventy guineas, he should avoid declaiming.[45]

Rhetorical dialogue, on the other hand, requires rhetorical speech, which is realistic delivery when a character is making a speech. Thus, in the passage between Tarleton and The Man (Gunner) in *Misalliance* –

> TARLETON.... you'll get no justice here: we dont keep it. Human nature is what we stock.
>
> THE MAN. Human nature! Debauchery! gluttony! selfishness! roberry of the poor! Is that what you call human nature?
>
> TARLETON. No: thats what you call it. Come, my lad! Whats the matter with you? You dont look starved; and youve a decent suit of clothes.

[42] Bernard Shaw, *Androcles and the Lion, Overruled, Pygmalion*, p. 162. The passage is from the preface to *Overruled*.

[43] *Shaw on Theatre*, p. 86.

[44] Copy of letter to Charles Charrington, March 4, 1900, British Museum, Add. 50532.

[45] Rehearsal notes: *Arms and the Man*, 1919, Burgunder Collection; *Pygmalion*, 1914, Hanley Collection.

THE MAN. Forty-two shillings.

TARLETON. They can do you a very decent suit for forty-two shillings.

– he advised Gunner, ' "Debauchery, selfishness, gluttony, robbery of the poor" – rhetoric, not realism – prepare for 42/-'. Despite Shaw's distinction between realism and rhetoric, and despite the obvious desire for a build so that Tarleton can get a laugh on his last speech, his request for a rhetorical delivery of Gunner's first speech is not inconsistent with realism. Because Gunner is pontificating, consciously making a speech for Tarleton's benefit, Shaw wanted him to be rhetorical. Again, when Sergius declares to Louka, 'Oh, (*fervently*) give me the man who will defy to the death any power on earth or in heaven that sets itself up against his own will and conscience: he alone is the brave man', Shaw urged the actor to 'Give it to the gallery – forget her'. These lines are, after all, the climax of an oratorical passage spoken by a man given to speechifying. Earlier in the speech, however, Shaw had Sergius cross downstage in order to 'avoid taking the stage at the end' of the speech.[46] The distinction is vital: to take the stage would be unrealistic, for Sergius is not an actor; but to deliver the speech as if he were giving it to the gallery would be realistic, for he is a man who breaks into declamation.

Although Shaw wanted realism, he also wanted his plays to be performed broadly. Calling his methods a 'throw-back to the art of Barry Sullivan and Italian opera', he requested 'the drunken, stagey, brassbowelled barnstormers my plays were written for', and exclaimed, 'Bumptiousness for me!'[47] Once, an actor who was cast as Burgess in *Candida* rehearsed the first act 'in subdued tones like a funeral mute'. As the author was about to protest, the actor 'solemnly put up his hand', saying, 'Mr Shaw: I know what you are going to say. But you may depend on me. In the intellectual drama I never clown.' Intellectual drama, the equation apparently

46 Rehearsal notes: *Misalliance*, 1910, Hanley Collection; *Arms and the Man*, 1911, Texas.

47 Letters: to Alan S. Downer, Nov. 12, 1947, in Meisel, *Shaw and the Nineteenth-Century Theater*, pp. 107-8; to Granville Barker, June 15, 1907, Jan. 19, 1908, in *Shaw-Barker*, pp. 93, 115.

went, meant serious drama, which called for a solemn attitude toward the role and an *ex cathedra* delivery of all speeches. 'It was some time', reports Shaw, 'before I could persuade him that I was in earnest when I exhorted him to clown for all he was worth. I was continually struggling with the conscientious efforts of our players to underdo their parts lest they should be considered stagey.'[48] The word 'underdone' occurs frequently in Shaw's rehearsal notes. Morrison's consternation at Undershaft's arrival was 'Underdone'. When Sergius touched the bruise on Louka's arm, causing her to flinch, both the stroke and the flinching were 'underdone'. At rehearsals of Lewis Casson's production of *Macbeth* in 1926, Shaw counselled Sybil Thorndike (Lady Macbeth) about the line, 'screw your courage to the sticking-place' (I, vii, 60), 'Dont soften – scold like a fury – underdone.'[49] Granville Barker, Shaw confessed, 'rebukes me feelingly for wanting my parts to be "caricatured" '. Shaw, on the other hand, chided Barker for underplaying, comparing him to Robert Loraine, who performs 'quite in my old-fashioned way, with a relish and not under protest, like you'.[50]

Shaw demanded that expansiveness and technical proficiency be part of a convincing performance.[51] But conviction, carried to its extreme, is total identification of the actor with the character. Did Shaw intend this? On the one hand, he wrote Ellen Terry that the only thing 'not forgivable in an actor is *being* the part instead of playing it'. As example, he pointed to Eleanora Duse's performance in Dumas *fils' La Femme de Claude,* in which she acts 'with an impossible perfection, and yet never touches the creature with the tips of her fingers'.[52] On the other hand, he said, 'On the highest plane one does not act, one *is.*' As examples, he pointed to Mrs Patrick Campbell's performances in John

[48] *Shaw on Theatre,* p. 221.

[49] Rehearsal notes: *Major Barbara,* 1935, British Museum, Add. 50644; *Arms and the Man,* 1911, Texas; *Macbeth,* 1926, British Museum, Add. 50644.

[50] Letters: to Henry Arthur Jones, Feb. 20, 1902, in Jones, *Taking the Curtain Call,* p. 178; to Granville Barker, May 24, 1907, in *Shaw-Barker,* p. 85.

[51] Letter to William Faversham, April 19, 1917, Hanley Collection.

[52] Letter to Ellen Terry, undated but assigned to July, 1897, in *Terry-Shaw,* p. 179.

Davidson's *For the Crown* and in Sheridan's *She Stoops to Conquer* (in which she played Lady Teazle). Yet he reviewed unfavourably a performance by Dorothea Baird which lacked this quality. Admitting that Miss Baird did precisely what the role demanded that she do, that she was 'letter-perfect, gesture-perfect, paint-perfect, dress-perfect, beauty-perfect, and imitation-pathos-perfect', he nevertheless concluded that 'if a play depends on the part being lived from the inside instead of put on as a shepherd putteth on his garment, then it will fail, though Miss Baird may seem to succeed'.[53] Although the familiar paradox of the actor being the character yet at the same time detached from the character might reconcile these apparently contradictory statements, Shaw did not explicitly reconcile them. He may have done so implicitly, however, by his demand that the actor have thorough control over everything he did.

THE ACTOR AND THE CHARACTER

As critic and as director, Shaw despised the actor's use of stage tricks, clichés, artificial indications of emotions the character is supposed to be feeling, posturing, posing – in general, anything destructive of the illusion of real things happening to real people. He defined 'character actor' as 'a clever stage performer who cannot act, and therefore makes an elaborate study of the disguises and stage tricks by which acting can be grotesquely simulated'.[54] As Mrs Alving in *Ghosts*, he maintained, Mrs Theodore Wright used such stage tricks: her 'application of the conventional stage method to the final situation, with advances and recoils and screams and general violent oscillations between No – yes – I cannot – I must &c&c&c, only proved, interestingly enough, that it cannot be done in that way'.[55] Olga Nethersole's performance in the title role of Arthur W. Pinero's *The Notorious Mrs Ebbsmith*, he wrote, was marked by posturing:

53 *Our Theatres in the Nineties*, II, 65, 171; III, 268-9.
54 *Ibid.*, I, 60.
55 Letter to Charles Charrington, March 30, 1891, in *Collected Letters*, p. 289.

When she pretends to darn a stocking she brings it down to the footlights, and poses in profile with the stockinged hand raised above the level of her head. She touches nothing without first poising her hand above it like a bird about to alight, or a pianist's fingers descending on a chord. She cannot even take up the box containing the rich dress to bundle it off into the next room, without disposing her hands round it with an unmistakeable reference to the conventional laws of grace.

Shaw objected to actors who played comedy by delivering all their lines and performing all their actions in high spirits, obstreperously, archly, with squawking voices and grinning faces intended ostentatiously to indicate their funniness. Once the audience becomes aware that an actor is trying to make an effect, the attempt fails. The actor whose performance does not portray the character, but merely describes him or suggests how the audience should react to him, will be applauded only 'by Partridge, with his "anybody can see that the king is an actor" '.[56] Because of this, Shaw frequently said that he wished actors would not 'act', by which he meant grotesque indicating rather than convincing representation. He implored Trebitsch to prevent Carl Wiene from 'acting' when Richard Dudgeon is arrested in the second act of *The Devil's Disciple:* 'Good God! imagine the idiot whispering and crying and "springing about", with the sergeant and the soldiers and the woman standing round admiring him like a Donizettian opera chorus!' When the sergeant arrests him, there must be complete silence. Richard should speak 'with frightful *quiet* distinctness', so that each of his words terrifies Judith. Then, after he turns and confronts a suspicious-looking sergeant, comes 'the great effect' when he gets the idea of having Judith kiss him in order to remove the sergeant's suspicion. 'All that will be utterly ruined if the damned scoundrel *acts*. He will want to act – to agonize, to make convulsive movements and play tricks with his voice. Do not let him. Tell him I say that he shall

[56] *Our Theatres in the Nineties*, I, 127-8, 214; II, 156; III, 196; *Shaw on Shakespeare*, ed. Edwin Wilson (New York: Dutton, 1961), p. 118.

not act. He may pray and fast and weep and go to confession; but *act*, by God, he shall not. I will have no monkey tricks in my play.'[57]

Shaw especially disapproved of the actor or actress who tried to secure personal admiration rather than to play the character. A prominent example was Sarah Bernhardt, whose dazzling appearance, he noted, seemed to say to the audience, 'Now who would ever suppose that I am a grandmother?' This effect, part of what he called 'the childishly egotistical character of her acting', was 'not the art of making you think more highly or feel more deeply, but the art of making you admire her, pity her, champion her, weep with her, laugh at her jokes, follow her fortunes breathlessly, and applaud her wildly when the curtain falls'. He regretted 'the shameless prostitution of the art of acting into the art of pleasing. The actor wants "sympathy": the actress wants affection. They make the theatre a place where the public comes to look at its pets and distributes lumps of sugar to them.' When the average actress was asked to play an 'unsympathetic' role, she refused to do so 'on exactly the same grounds as she might refuse to let her lover see her in curlpapers. And the actors are worse than the actresses.' As a critic, he objected to an actress who played an elderly lady but refused to conceal the fact that she was young.[58] As a director, he worried that the actress portraying Mrs Higgins wanted to avoid appearing middle-aged.[59] As a critic, he objected to Mrs Patrick Campbell's removal of the unpleasant aspects of *Little Eyolf* in an attempt to secure admiration of her charm, beauty, and self-possession.[60] As a director, he insisted that Mrs Campbell refrain from making 'a sympathetic point' in *Pygmalion* when Higgins remarks that at times he would call her attractive.[61]

Shaw admired the actor who played the character, instead of

[57] Letter to Siegfried Trebitsch, Jan. 10, 1903, Berg Collection.
[58] *Our Theatres in the Nineties*, I, 149-50; II, 52, 283.
[59] Letter to Mrs Patrick Campbell, Jan. 29, 1920, in *Shaw-Campbell*, p. 232.
[60] *Our Theatres in the Nineties*, II, 272-3.
   Rehearsal notes, *Pygmalion*, 1914, Hanley Collection.

substituting himself or his stage self for that character. He accused Henry Irving of having had 'only one part; and that part was the part of Irving. His Hamlet was not Shakespear's Hamlet, nor his Lear Shakespear's Lear: they were both avatars of the imaginary Irving in whom he was so absorbingly interested.' Sometimes this was an improvement, at other times a disgrace. 'His Iachimo, a very fine performance, was better than Shakespear's Iachimo, and not a bit like him. On the other hand, his Lear was in impertinent intrusion of a quite silly conceit of his own into a great play.' Irving did not adapt himself to the role he played: '. . . his creations were all his own; and they were all Irvings.' By comparison, Ellen Terry played 'Beatrice, Juliet, Portia, Imogen, etc., intelligently and charmingly just as Shakespear planned them. . . '. Similarly, he contrasted Sarah Bernhardt and Eleanora Duse. Like Irving, Bernhardt 'does not enter into the leading character: she substitutes herself for it'. With Duse, as with Ellen Terry, 'every part is a separate creation'.[62]

Shaw did distinguish between 'the actor's tendency to adapt the play to his own personality and the author's desire to adapt the actor's personality to the play'.[63] Acting, he advised Laurence Irving, 'must always depend on the success of the pretence that the character is you, not on the pretence that you are the character – the amateur's notion . . .'.[64] The distinction is subtle but important. The actor who pretends that he is the character imagines himself in the situation the author has imagined, and so behaves as he himself might behave, thus adapting the play to his own personality. The character then becomes an embodiment of him, rather than he of the character. On the other hand, the actor who pretends that the character is himself tries to find the aspects of himself which will elucidate and embody the character, adapting his personality to the play. In 1889, Shaw declared that while there had been only one genuine clown, Grimaldi, 'we all have a clown in us somewhere; and Garrick's Petruchio, Lemaître's

---

62 *Pen Portraits and Reviews*, pp. 163, 169; *Our Theatres in the Nineties*, I, 149.
63 *Pen Portraits and Reviews*, p. 276.
64 Letter to Laurence Irving, Dec. 26, 1900, Houghton Library, Harvard College.

Macaire, and Mr Irving's Jingle and Jeremy Diddler may be regarded as the outcome of the impulse felt by these actors to realize for a moment the clown in themselves'.[65] Shaw would prefer that the actor try to find the role in himself, rather than merely trying to play himself in the role.

The printed texts of his plays contain character descriptions designed to help the actor play the character the author drew. The *'stout and fatherly'* Father Dempsey, for example, in *John Bull's Other Island,* is described as falling

> *far short of that finest type of countryside pastor which represents the genius of priesthood; but he is equally far above the base type in which a strongminded unscrupulous peasant uses the Church to extort money, power, and privilege. He is a priest neither by vocation nor ambition, but because the life suits him. He has boundless authority over his flock, and taxes them stiffly enough to be a rich man. The old Protestant ascendancy is now too broken to gall him. On the whole, an easygoing, amiable, even modest man as long as his dues are paid and his authority and dignity fully admitted.*

Characterization is not simply a matter of a few stock attitudes. Shaw criticized Evelyn Millard's performance as Pinero's *The Second Mrs Tanqueray* for merely dividing the role into sympathetic passages and outbursts of temper, and then shifting quickly from the one to the other. Nor is characterization a matter of a few 'points'. The beginner, says Shaw, will find several points in a role, play them, and, in between, allow the role to play itself. When these points are smoothly executed, he will invent more points, executing them more smoothly and forcefully. After a time, he will continually make points. With some, this is the final stage. 'But with the greatest artists there soon commences an integration of the points into a continuous whole, at which stage the [actor] appears to make no points at all, and to proceed in the most unstudied and "natural" way.'[66]

65 Bernard Shaw, *Platform and Pulpit*, ed. Dan H. Laurence (New York: Hill and Wang, 1961), p. 17.
66 *Our Theatres in the Nineties*, I, 146-7, 168.

But characterization, Shaw maintained, involves more than this. It means understanding the sort of person the playwright has created, and using this understanding as a guide to his actions and behaviour. As a director, Shaw tried to help the actor achieve this understanding. Coaching Ellen Terry for the role of Imogen in *Cymbeline*, he first described the character in general terms: 'Imogen is an impulsive person, with quick transitions, absolutely frank self-expression, and no half affections or half forgivenesses.' Following this, he explained general behavioural characteristics: 'The moment you abuse anyone she loves, she is in a rage: the moment you praise them she is delighted.' With these observations in mind, he interpreted specific scenes in Act II:

> It is quite easy for Iachimo to put her out of countenance by telling her that Posthumus has forgotten her; but the instant he makes the mistake of trying to gratify her by abusing him – 'that runagate' – he brings down the avalanche. It is just the same with Cloten: she is forbearing with him until he makes the same mistake. And Iachimo has nothing to do but praise Posthumus, and lay the butter on thick, and she is instantly as pleased as Punch, and void of all resentment. It is this that makes her pay him the extra special compliment of offering to take the chest into her own bedroom, *a thing she would never have done if she had not forgiven him* quite thoroughly – honest Injun.[67]

In commenting to actors about his own characters, he frequently wanted to convey an impression about the sort of person that was being represented. He told Sybil Thorndike that Joan of Arc was nineteen years old, not a child or an angelically sweet little girl, but a sturdy woman.[68] Trying to create a similar image for Wendy Hiller, he advised her not to rub her ankle pathetically when the chain was removed, but rather to 'bend your legs at the knee and stretch them as if you were going to take on the whole court at all-in wrestling. And call the man a noodle heartily, not

[67] Letter to Ellen Terry, Sept. 8, 1896, in *Terry-Shaw*, p. 46.
[68] Interview with Dame Sybil Thorndike, June 29, 1964.

peevishly, get a big laugh at it.'[69] He explained certain aspects of *Major Barbara* to Annie Russell:

> 'Nonsense! of course its funny' might be a little more peremptory. There are one or two points like the 'Nonsense! she must do as she's told' (about Rummy) in which Barbara, with all her sweetness, shews that she is her mother's daughter, and that it comes very natural to her to order people about. There is a curious touch of aristocratic pride at the very end, where she says she does not want to die in God's debt, and will forgive him 'as becomes a woman of her rank' for all the starvation and mischief he is responsible for. Barbara has great courage, great pride and a high temper at the back of her religious genius; and you need not hesitate to let them flash through at moments if any of the passages catch you that way.[70]

To Irene Vanbrugh, he described the Polish aviatrix Lina as 'the St Joan of Misalliance': she is not a thrill-hunter but 'a religious force'. Trained as an acrobat, she devotes herself to dangerous exercises but 'has a nun's grave disapproval of stunts that are not really either difficult or dangerous . . .'. Her dedication, however, is coupled with independence:

> . . . she is very like a modern nun except that her sexual morality is not that of the church: marriage is to her a sale of herself: she must be free. Her stage foundation is a grave and almost mystical beauty; and Tarleton has the surprise of his life when, touched by it, he finds that he cant buy it, even for love. . . .
>
> When she takes Bentley she is devoting him to death, as she devotes herself every day. Something of that should be felt by the audience; for it is to that that Bentley responds. It is a hieratic act on her part.[71]

---

[69] Copy of letter to Wendy Hiller, Aug. 17, 1936, courtesy Miss Hiller.

[70] Letter to Annie Russell, Nov. 20, 1905, Manuscript Room, New York Public Library.

[71] Letter to Irene Vanbrugh, March 26, 1930, in Irene Vanbrugh, *To Tell My Story* (London: Hutchinson, 1950), pp. 205-6.

Comments such as these can be extremely helpful to the actresses playing Joan, Barbara, and Lina, for they contain precise images that can be translated into behaviour.

For Shaw, characterization was incomplete unless the actor understood the class characteristics of the person he played. After attending a performance of *Captain Brassbound's Conversion*, for instance, he informed Janet Achurch that she would be unable to play Lady Cicely convincingly until she had completed 'a careful study of the English lady. Mind: I dont mean the English bourgeoise, nor the English artist-Bohemian; I mean the great lady.' Shaw claimed that he, like Molière, consulted his cook about his plays. According to the cook, according to Shaw, when Janet Achurch 'sat down she got her dress tucked in between her knees: no high lady would do that'. Heartily agreeing with his cook's criticism, he told the actress that she played the entire role with her dress tucked between her knees. A great lady, he observed,

> would hardly ever shew real excitement, or lose her distinction and immense self-complacency and habit of patronage. . . . She might be childish, and make little jokes and puns that only courtiers laugh at; she might even go on with men in a way which in a shop-girl would lead to overtures and be understood to have that intention; she might do forty thousand things that no woman who was not either above or below suspicion would do (the coincidences between the tramp and the aristocrat are very interesting); but in everything external she would be distinguished from the middle-class woman, who lives her whole life under suspicion and shortness of cash.

Until Miss Achurch had mastered all of these marks of caste, and could imitate them as easily as she could distinguish between one shade of grease paint and another, she would be unable to act Lady Cicely. 'It is not that court ladylikeness is difficult; but it is antipathetic to the free Bohemian middle-class *revoltée*: the essence of it is flunkeyism, upper-servantism', which she must study dispassionately until she was able to perform it mechanically.[72]

Shaw's intent was to relate social to psychological realism. The social themes of modern plays, especially those of Ibsen, create difficulties for the actor accustomed to the English theatre's stock characters, which are often based on moral judgments. Puzzled by Ibsen's high-minded characters whose high-mindedness causes mischief, the conventional actor assumes that if a stage character is selfish, he must be a villain; if self-sacrificing, a hero; and if unconsciously ridiculous, a comedian. Not only do these assumptions reduce Ibsen's characters to stage stereotypes, but they are impossible to execute in a satisfactory manner. It is difficult for an actor or actress to be laughed at while playing a serious part, such as Gregers Werle in *The Wild Duck*, but this is exactly what Ibsen demands: his plays expose the very conventions upon which the actor bases his conceptions of stock types. Ibsen does not distribute sympathy according to traditional moralistic assumptions. He makes 'lost' women lovable, portraying them as compassionate *because* they are 'lost' and giving them the sympathy that usually goes to the righteous character. Moreover, by having women describe men as 'lost' and 'ruined', he ridicules such moralistic terms. Ibsen cannot, therefore, be played from the conventional viewpoint. His characters must be portrayed from their own points of view. This, in fact, is a consistent Shavian principle: dramas that deal realistically with modern men and women cannot be presented according to conventional stage conceptions; rather, they must be played from the viewpoint of the characters' own conceptions of themselves.[73]

Shaw was not satisfied with mere descriptive acting. He praised James Pursail for noticing that, 'as [Don Giovanni] was not a professional singer, however masterfully he may sing all the dramatic music, he should sing the serenade like an amateur. And this was just what Mr Pursail did. I do not mean that he sang it badly: on the contrary, he sang it very nicely . . . I mean that

---

[72] Letter to Janet Achurch, Dec. 26, 1900, in *Shaw on Theatre*, pp. 81-3.
[73] *Shaw on Theatre*, pp. 1-3; *Our Theatres in the Nineties*, II, 4-5.

Mr Pursail sang it, not in the traditionally ardent and accomplished manner, but in the manner of a modest amateur.'[74] Shaw's advice to Janet Achurch on playing Candida had a similar basis: although dignity must underlie all of Candida's behaviour, 'the least attempt on your part to be dignified will be utterly fatal'.[75] The actress, in other words, should behave as the character would behave. Candida does not try to *be* dignified: she *is* dignified. The quality should not be described for the benefit of the audience, or paraded as if it were an elaborate accomplishment, but taken for granted and allowed to underlie her behaviour.

As a director, Shaw tried to prevent the actor from inserting business which was inconsistent with the character – warning Straker, for example, 'not to touch his hat' to Violet in the fourth act of *Man and Superman* (had he not told Tanner in the second act that his grandfather, but not he, would have touched his hat to members of the upper class?). Alert to the danger of the actor substituting his own reaction for the character's reaction, Shaw told Stephen not to laugh at Lady Britomart's laugh-lines, even though the audience may do so; instead, he should maintain 'a strain of seriousness . . . all through'. When Raina reacts to Bluntschli's description of Sergius leading the cavalry charge 'like an operatic tenor', the actress must realize that Raina 'likes an operatic tenor'.[76]

In comedy too, the actor should maintain the character's viewpoint and not play for laughs (unless, of course, the character himself is trying to be amusing). Shaw assured directors of *John Bull's Other Island* that Broadbent 'will get endless laughs until he begins to play for them', but warned that 'With the exception of the stage Irishman in the first act [Tim Haffigan], the performers must not speak as if it were funny to be Irish and speak with an Irish accent'.[77] Broadbent and the Irishmen in Acts II, III, and

[74] *How to Become a Musical Critic*, p. 301.
[75] Letter to Janet Achurch, March 20, 1895, in *Collected Letters*, p. 502.
[76] Rehearsal notes: *Man and Superman*, 1907, British Museum, Add. 50735; *Major Barbara*, 1905, British Museum, Add. 50733; *Arms and the Man*, 1911, Texas.
[77] 'Instructions to The Producer [of *John Bull's Other Island*]', typed manuscript, dated 'Christmas 1904', British Museum, Add. 50615.

IV are unconsciously funny, whereas Tim Haffigan, deliberately playing the stereotyped comic Irishman, is trying to amuse and to ingratiate himself. Most of the company of the 1919 revival of *Arms and the Man*, noted Shaw, played for laughs, and thus produced 'that detestable effect . . . of all the characters being so many Shaws spouting Shavianisms, and provoking first a lot of shallow but willing laughter, and then producing disappointment and irritation'. The antidote, he told Robert Loraine, was to ignore the audience and play the characters in the situation.[78] His rehearsal notes contain similar injunctions. When Liza talks of her father ladling gin down her mother's throat, Higgins must not laugh but must behave as though drops of sweat were pouring down his brow[79] (for he is anxious during his pupil's first encounter with cultivated people). Shaw also warned that unless 'Not bloody likely' is said in perfect seriousness, unconscious of the fact that it may produce a laugh, it will ruin the play.[80]

Thus, the actor should be believable as the character. Avoiding clichés, posturing, and artificial indications of emotion, he should play not himself but a fully individualized character responding to a particular situation, behaving as that character would behave, and playing the role from the character's point of view.

MOTIVATION

In its obvious sense, stage motivation means that the actor should have a reason for what he does. It implies that the audience should perceive that he has one. The absence of motivation is the basis of many of Shaw's rehearsal notes, which record, for instance, that the General (*Getting Married*) should motivate his sitting down, and that Liza's 'Slow walk' is 'not motivated'.[81] He warns the actor against anticipating the business or the line to which he

[78] Letter to Robert Loraine, Dec. 14, 1919, in Winifred Loraine, *Head Wind: The Story of Robert Loraine* (New York: Morrow, n.d.), pp. 268-71.
[79] Rehearsal notes, *Pygmalion*, 1914, Hanley Collection.
[80] Letter to George C. Tyler, Oct. 11, 1914, in Mander and Mitchenson, *Theatrical Companion to Shaw*, p. 160.
[81] Rehearsal notes: *Getting Married*, 1908, Enthoven Collection; *Pygmalion*, 1914, Hanley Collection.

reacts: the cause must come before the result. When Higgins is reminded by the church clock that he should be charitable to the flower-girl, he must not get out his money before the clock strikes.[82] Leo (*Getting Married*) should not anticipate Reginald's line 'You damned scoundrel, how dare you throw my wife over like that before my face', which is her cue for preventing him from assaulting Hotchkiss: earlier, she had no inkling of his intentions.[83]

In order for the actor to show his reasons for speaking and acting, he should first understand them. Some of Shaw's rehearsal notes explain the motivation: he told Hotchkiss, for example, that when the Bishop says ' "soldiers & servants" – this is where he recognizes the baptism service. Up to that he is at a loss'.[84] In his letters to actors, Shaw combined statements on motivation with prescriptions on externals. He advised Louis Calvert:

> In the scene with Cusins (the drum scene) you must be on the lookout for 'Not Paganism either, eh?' 'I admit that,' because the next speech, 'You have noticed that she is original in her religion' comes with sudden force and pride. Indeed, the change comes from the line 'And now to business'. Up to that, Undershaft has been studying Cusins and letting him talk. But the shake-hands means that he has made up his mind that Cusins is the man to understand him; and he therefore takes the lead in the conversation and dominates Cusins at once.[85]

Not only did Shaw explain why Undershaft has been allowing Cusins to expound on the activities of the Salvation Army and to declaim passages from *The Bacchae*, he also prescribed the manner in which a speech should be given and described the effect of Undershaft's change of manner. The motivational and non-motivational advice are linked. In his advice to Matthew Boulton,

---

[82] Rehearsal notes, *Pygmalion*, 1914, Hanley Collection.

[83] Rehearsal notes, *Getting Married*, 1908, Enthoven Collection.

[84] *Ibid.*

[85] Letter to Louis Calvert, Nov. 27, 1905, in 'George Bernard Shaw as a Man of Letters', p. 6.

who played Boanerges in *The Apple Cart*, they were more clearly differentiated:

> B. comes to court with a powerful conception of himself as a man of the people leading them in the struggle against the governing classes. All the Boanergeses do. The notion that there is no governing *class* – that government is carried on by the strong men, no matter what class they belong to, and that his lot is with the strong men and not with the people (whether he is on their side or not), is quite new to him, though everything he has been saying to the king about democracy proves it. Consequently the princess's 'anyone can see that you belong to the governing class' is a flash of revelation to him. I have given him no dialogue to express this: it has to come out between the lines; but every time I see it I feel that he *must* play to it. I cannot make him exclaim 'Yes, by God! it's true' because it would run the scene right off the rails; but [it] can be done quite easily by suddenly unfolding the arms, opening the mouth, and lifting the eyes at the cue 'governing class'. Just try it. You will find yourself doing it involuntarily when you get the idea.[86]

Here, Shaw first explained Boanerges' motivation: his conception of himself and his internal reaction to what is told him. Then, he suggested physical, external business to convey the character's thoughts.

As his advice to Matthew Boulton suggests, Shaw was concerned with motivation not only in its obvious sense but also in its sense of revealing a character's thoughts and desires – his 'inner life'. In one of his theatre reviews he wrote, 'I suspect that Miss [Violet] Vanbrugh has hitherto lamed herself by trying to arrive at Miss Ellen Terry's secret from without inward, instead of working out her own secret from within outward.'[87] As a director, he worked on both approaches.

86 Letter to Matthew Boulton, Sept. 1, 1929, The Philbrick Library, Los Altos Hills, Calif.
87 *Our Theatres in the Nineties*, II, 151.

To help the actor understand the character, Shaw sometimes used models and images. On one occasion, he told Sybil Thorndike that Joan of Arc was like a suffragette. At times he would name a specific person as a model, suggesting that the actor imitate him.[88] The actor playing Cusins in *Major Barbara*, he told Theresa Helburn, should use Gilbert Murray as a model; if he had never seen Murray, the next best model was Harold Lloyd. Granville Barker, who acted the role in London, was asked to play Puck to Louis Calvert's Mephistopheles. Apollodorus' dive into the sea in *Caesar and Cleopatra*, Shaw wrote Gabriel Pascal, might make Caesar 'so excited ... that he snatches off his helmet and hurls it at Britannus like a ball at cricket; and Britannus fields it like a first-class wicket-keeper'.[89] He told Beerbohm Tree that 'Tosh, Eliza' should be 'Miltonic', and suggested that Mrs Patrick Campbell use the image 'Blind terror of a hunted animal' when Higgins reproduces her words and accent.[90]

Shaw also tried to make visual both character relationships and motivations which come from other characters. In the third act of *John Bull's Other Island*, for example, Matt Haffigan tells Father Dempsey, 'If I might make so bould, Fadher, I wouldnt say but an English Prodestn mighnt have a more indepindent mind about the lan, an be less afeerd to spake out about it dhan an Irish Catholic.' Shaw told the actor to wait after 'If I might make so bould, father' ... [until you get] leave to speak'. Later in the act, Larry Doyle responds to Matt Haffigan's calling him a turncoat:

LARRY. St Peter, the rock on which our Church was built, was crucified head downwards for being a turncoat.
FATHER DEMPSEY (*with a quiet authoritative dignity which checks Doran, who is on the point of breaking out*) Thats true.

---

[88] Interview with Dame Sybil Thorndike, June 29, 1964.
[89] Letters: to Theresa Helburn, 1928 (no month or day given), in Langner, *G.B.S.*, p. 110; to Granville Barker, Aug. 3, 1905, in *Shaw-Barker*, p. 50; to Gabriel Pascal, July 9, 1944, in Marjorie Deans, *Meeting at the Sphinx: Gabriel Pascal's Production of Bernard Shaw's Caesar and Cleopatra* (London: Macdonald, n.d.), p. 41.
[90] Rehearsal notes, *Pygmalion*, 1914, Hanley Collection.

You hold your tongue as befits your ignorance, Matthew Haffigan. . . .

After 'Thats true', Matt was asked to open his mouth in order to motivate the priest's next line. In *Caesar and Cleopatra*, Cleopatra is provoked to jealousy when Caesar asks her brother,

CAESAR . . . . Come here, my boy, and stand by me.
Ptolemy goes over to Caesar, who, resuming his seat on the tripod, takes the boy's hand to encourage him. Cleopatra, furiously jealous, rises and glares at them.
CLEOPATRA (*with flaming cheeks*) Take your throne: I dont want it. (*She flings away the chair, and approaches Ptolemy, who shrinks from her.*)

In order to explain the fury of Cleopatra's jealousy, Shaw noted during rehearsal that more was needed than Caesar's line: '. . . there must be some petting by Caesar. REHEARSE.' In *Arms and the Man*, Bluntschli draws up orders and then passes them to Sergius, who signs them with difficulty. In the 1894 typescript (and also in the first edition of *Plays Pleasant*), he signs '*with the air of a man resolutely performing a difficult and dangerous feat*'. In the Standard Edition (1931), prepared after the play had been produced several times, Shaw made this 'air' visual: Sergius '*signs with his cheek on his elbow and his protruded tongue following the movements of his pen*'. Following the signature (in all versions), Sergius tells Bluntschli, 'This hand is more accustomed to the sword than to the pen.' During rehearsals of the 1911 production, Shaw had Bluntschli provoke the explanation by reacting to Sergius' manner of signing his name: 'When Serg lays his head on his arm to sign, look at him in alarm.'[91]

The stage directions in the printed editions of Shaw's plays help give the actor motivation for what he says and does. In the third act of *Widowers' Houses*, for instance, Blanche tells Trench, 'I dont want you to stay.' Then:

[91] Rehearsal notes: *John Bull's Other Island,* undated, Hanley Collection; *Caesar and Cleopatra*, 1912, Texas; *Arms and the Man,* 1911, Texas.

> *For a moment they stand face to face, quite close to one another,*
> *she provocative, taunting, half defying, half inviting him to advance,*
> *in a flush of undisguised animal excitement. It suddenly flashes on*
> *him that all this ferocity is erotic: that she is making love to him.*
> *His eye lights up: a cunning expression comes into the corners of his*
> *mouth: with a heavy assumption of indifference he walks straight*
> *to his chair, and plants himself in it with his arms folded.*

A clear description of the characters' motivation, this stage
direction prompts the remainder of Blanche's speech. In *Man and
Superman,* when Starker accuses Mendoza of funk, the latter
springs to his feet, telling Enry that he comes from 'a famous
family of fighters' and that Enry 'would have as much chance
against me as a perambulator against your motor car'. Though
Straker says, 'I aint afraid of you,' a stage direction reveals that
he is *'secretly daunted, but [rises] from his knees with an air of
reckless pugnacity'.* The subtext, implicit in the text, is often
explicit in the stage directions.

As a director too, Shaw attended to subtext. Advising Ellen
Terry how to play Imogen, he persuaded her that her speech after
Posthumus puts a bracelet upon her arm – 'O the gods! / When
shall we see again?' (I, i, 123-24) –

> is really two separate speeches. When Posthumus puts the
> bracelet on your arm, look for a moment with delight at the
> present if you like, but that doesnt matter: the great thing is
> that you shiver with love at his touch on your arm, and say
> 'O the gods!' as a sigh of rapture. It is when that subsides that
> you ask the question a woman always does ask – it being the
> nature of her sex never to be satisfied – 'When will you come
> again?'

He also suggested that in the same scene, her speech to Cymbeline
– I beseech you, sir, / Harm not yourself with your vexation' (lines
133-34) – should be 'thoroughly petulant and full of temper,
Cymbeline having not only sent Posthumus away, but called

him "thou basest thing". What she really means is "You may save your breath to cool your porridge, you old wretch" '.[92] Shaw continually tried to enrich the text by helping the actor understand and express the subtext, or 'What she really means'. When he assisted Lewis Casson in the direction of *Macbeth*, he noted that when Macbeth said, 'If I stand here, I saw him [Banquo's ghost]' (III, iv, 74), there should be more 'relief . . . at the vanishing'. In *Pygmalion*, when Mrs Pearce tells Higgins that they must be 'very particular with this girl as to personal cleanliness. . . . I mean not to be slovenly about her dress or untidy in leaving things about', Higgins agrees and turns to Pickering, saying, 'It is these little things that matter, Pickering. Take care of the pence and the pounds will take care of themselves is as true of personal habits as of money.' Shaw suggested to Higgins, 'Imply that Pick is careless of his person.'[93]

In his concern for motivation, and for internal reality, Shaw wanted the actor to achieve a moment-to-moment reality, to 'think on his feet', as it were, and give the illusion that events were happening to him for the first time. 'An actor's cue', he maintained, 'is not a signal to take up the running thoughtlessly, but a provocation to retort or respond in some clearly differentiated way. He must, even on the thousandth night, make the audience believe that he has never heard his cue before.'[94] As a critic, he berated Lewis Waller for having 'delivered his lines with the automatic gravity of a Brompton Cemetery clergyman repeating the burial service for the thousandth time', and reprimanded Mrs Patrick Campbell for having delivered a long speech 'as a schoolgirl repeats her catechism: its happy indifference of manner and glib utterance almost unhinged my reason'.[95] As a director, he warned Candida that certain responses were 'too glib' and asked Malcolm not to rattle off the string of epithets he heaps on Macbeth:

92 Letter to Ellen Terry, Sept. 8, 1896, in *Terry-Shaw*, p. 47.
93 Rehearsal notes: *Macbeth*, 1926, British Museum, Add. 50644; *Pygmalion*, 1920, 1920, British Museum, Add. 50644.
94 *Shaw on Theatre*, p. 157.
95 *Our Theatres in the Nineties*, I, 254; III, 53.

> I grant him bloody,
> Luxurious, avaricious, false, deceitful,
> Sudden, malicious, smacking of every sin
> That has a name.[96]

(IV, iii, 57-60)

Often, his advice contained specific suggestions to help the actor convey the impression that he was speaking his lines for the first time. Macbeth's response to the Witches addressing him as Thane of Cawdor and King was 'too prompt – not puzzled enough'. When Raina asks Bluntschli to tell her about the cavalry charge, Shaw noted that he is at first 'Rather puzzled at how to describe it'. Actors who must describe something, Shaw pointed out, should not have the adjectives ready to hand, but should let the audience see them trying to find the right words. When Percival (*Misalliance*) mentions the possibility of asking a woman to share his 'degrading poverty', he should 'pick out "degrading"'.[97] And if Baudricourt (*Saint Joan*) 'goes for PACE and picks up his cues smartly, evidently knowing all about them beforehand, he will ruin the first scene. Everything that Joan says to him takes him aback. . . . He is trying to bully her; but she counters all his leads in an utterly unexpected way. She always *surprises* him.'[98] This moment-to-moment reality, acting and reacting as if events were occurring and words spoken for the first time, helps to achieve the illusion of real things happening to real people.

Shaw insisted that the actor dissect the individual speech as well as the scene, breaking it down into small, precise, and clearly differentiated units, each with a separate meaning and purpose. As a critic, he objected to a singer in *Das Rheingold*: 'Every line he uttered was exactly like every other line.'[99] As a director, he tried to guard against this. In *You Never Can Tell*, Crampton's

---

[96] Rehearsal notes: *Candida*, 1920, British Museum, Add. 50644; *Macbeth*, 1926, British Museum, Add. 50644.
[97] Rehearsal notes: *Macbeth*, 1926, British Museum, Add. 50644; *Arms and the Man*, 1911, British Museum, Add. 50644; *Misalliance*, 1910, Hanley Collection.
[98] Letter to B.B.C., Sept. 1, 1941, Burgunder Collection.
[99] *Music in London*, II, 125.

' "She told you what I am – a father – a father robbed of his children" is all right as a frantic retort to Valentine, but . . . he must then collapse, and begin "What are the hearts of this generation" brooding brokenheartedly to himself'.[100] When Dubedat admits that he pawned Walpole's cigarette case – 'It's quite safe: he cant sell it for a year, you know. I say, my dear Walpole, I a m sorry' – he should 'get the change' between the sentences. Macbeth's line about Banquo's heirs – 'To make them kings, the seed of Banquo kings!' (III, i, 70) – should be delivered: ' "to make them kings." Change – "the seed of B. kings!!!" '[101]

In a letter to John L. Shine, he gave detailed instructions on breaking down Larry Doyle's long speech in the first act of *John Bull's Other Island*:

BROADBENT. The usual thing in the country, Larry. Just the same here.

LARRY (not too quick, and shaking his head) No, no: the climate is different. Here (in this sanguinary England), if the life is dull, you can be dull too, and no harm done. (Laughter at the expense of English dulness. So far, shew no sign that there is a long speech coming; and keep your eye on Louis [Calvert as Broadbent], or he'll immediately bung a corruscation of some kind, probably out of the fourth act).

(Now go right into sheer poetry with) 'But your wits cant thicken &c' down to 'dreaming dreaming'. Get back to prose in the 'No debauchery' sentence by a shiver of disgust and a nervous fidget; and then turn to Broadbent and *tell* him about 'An Irishman's imagination' – rub it into him, the climax being your quoting his own words 'agreeable to strangers'. Then add bitterly and with a sort of half tender reproach to him 'like a good-for-nothing woman on the streets', meaning 'A nice compliment to pay me, Tom: to tell me that I have the accomplishment of a whore – *agreeable to strangers*'.

Then comes 'Its all dreaming – all imagination', which you

100 Letter to Granville Barker, July 19, 1906, in *Shaw-Barker*, p. 65.
101 Rehearsal notes: *The Doctor's Dilemma*, 1913, Texas; *Macbeth*, 1926, British Museum, Add. 50644.

have got all right. It brings you quite back to cool description, which you need not trouble about, as the audience will be satisfied with the political interest of what you are saying, and will perhaps laugh at Yeats's expense when you mention Kathleen ni Houlihan.

Then you get back to work again on 'It saves thinking'. Go ahead angrily, contemptuously, disgustedly, but not poetically; and finish on 'useless devils like yourself'.

Now comes your final section. At 'And all the while' you drop your voice in a sort of horrible shame, because you are no longer describing what the other people do, but remembering what you did yourself. Get the change right; and your talent will pull you through the rest without any further suggestion, the last part of the speech being poetic and emotional.

I think this will help you to get command of the speech, and sufficient variety to save you from the feeling of holding on to it for dear life and not being able to stop yourself. But dont worry yourself by trying in any way to carry out my suggestions exactly or hampering yourself in any way with them. Very likely when you study them over you will be able to improve on them.[102]

Employing explanatory paraphrase ('Here' means 'in this sanguinary England'), mechanical business ('a shiver of disgust and a nervous fidget'), subtext ('a sort of half tender reproach'), literary analysis (poetry, prose, and description), and inner feeling (shame when he remembers what he himself did), Shaw's analysis separates the speech into distinct units – not *always* in motivational terms, to be sure, but nevertheless designed to create variety and assist the illusion that a character is formulating and enunciating his thoughts step by step, moment by moment, to another character, instead of repeating a set speech.

When the actor was in a scene with several characters, Shaw asked him to dissect his speeches so that he demonstrated different

[102] Letter to John L. Shine, Oct. 29, 1904, Hanley Collection.

attitudes toward each of them. On Macbeth's 'How does your patient, doctor?' (V, iii, 37), spoken immediately after ordering Seyton to scour the country and kill defeatists, Shaw urged, 'contrast to order to Seyton'. Similarly, he suggested that Higgins provide a 'Contrast between speech to Pick[ering] & speech to Liza'.[103]

Another factor in establishing a feeling of reality is the actor's awareness of and reaction to physical conditions. Shaw apparently missed this quality in the James Hackett – Mrs Patrick Campbell *Macbeth*, for he wrote to Mrs Campbell, 'You should not have forgotten that there was blood on your hands and on his, and that you dared not touch one another for fear of messing your clothes with gore.'[104] He advised Higgins not to throw Liza's hat on the piano, for that action 'would shake the creepy crawlies out of it', and reminded Louka that since her arm had been bruised by Sergius' grasp, 'Dont forget the sore arm in crossing arms.'[105] An awareness of mood and milieu also helps make the action credible. The beginning of *Misalliance*, for instance, should not be too rapid, for it is a 'Lazy afternoon'.[106] The actor must be alert not only to the time of day, but also to other characters who might influence his behaviour. 'Dont *slam* the window when youre running away,' he advised Ellen Terry, who was playing the title role in *Olivia*; 'the Vicar might hear you'.[107]

Shaw also wanted the actor to be constantly aware of – and reacting to – the other actors on stage. Throughout his rehearsal notes, he told actors to 'play to' – meaning, 'react to' – a line or action. Sometime he simply indicated that there should be a response. When Shotover (*Heartbreak House*) replies to Ellie Dunn's statement that her father is not a pirate but a good man, maintaining, 'He must be greatly changed', Ellie should 'Play to

103 Rehearsal notes: *Macbeth*, 1926, British Museum, Add. 50644; *Pygmalion*, 1914, Hanley Collection.
104 Letter to Mrs Patrick Campbell, Dec. 22, 1920, in *Shaw-Campbell*, pp. 245-6.
105 Rehearsal notes: *Pygmalion*, 1914, Hanley Collection; *Arms and the Man*, 1911, British Museum, Add. 50644.
106 Rehearsal notes, *Misalliance*, 1910, Hanley Collection.
107 Letter to Ellen Terry, Jan. 31, 1897, The Philbrick Library, Los Altos Hills, Calif.

this'. And when Undershaft testifies that he has conscientious scruples against attending prayer services, Lady Britomart should 'play to "conscientious scruples" '. Sometimes, Shaw indicated *how* the characters should react. After Candida calls Morell 'a thorough clergyman', he replies, 'So Eugene says'; Shaw asked her to react to his line with 'surprise & delight'. Nicola's 'We shall have our evenings to ourselves' should cause Louka to 'shudder at the prospect'. The uncomprehending Liza should greet Higgins' explanation of the uses of a handkerchief with a 'vacant stare'.[108] Shaw sometimes noted the motivation for a response. Tanner's comment on 'The New Man' is 'new to Straker'. When Catherine tells Petkoff that the blue closet contains his raincoat, her overcoat, and two old dressing gowns belonging to their daughter, Raina 'Doesnt like her two old dressing-gowns being mentioned'.[109]

As the note about Raina's dressing-gown indicates, Shaw the director attended to the responses of characters not engaged in the dialogue. During Ramsden's statement to Ann (*Man and Superman*), 'Suppose you were to discover that I had been guilty of some disgraceful action – that I was not the man your poor dear father took me for', Tavy should 'play to the "disgraceful action" '. Ross's announcement (*Macbeth*, I, ii, 62) that the Norwegian King has disbursed 'Ten thousand dollars to our general use' should prompt a general reaction: "10,000 dollars" – all play to it'.[110]

This was part of Shaw's desire to help establish a feeling of ensemble among the actors. He suggested the interpolation of business in order to assist the actors in creating the sense of give and take so crucial to realistic acting. In *Misalliance*, Tarleton confesses that he has a yen for Lina, which prompts Summerhays to remind him that she is his guest; Tarleton

[108] Rehearsal notes: *Heartbreak House*, 1921, Burgunder Collection; *Major Barbara*, 1935, British Museum, Add. 50644; *Candida*, 1920, British Museum, Add. 50644; *Arms and the Man*, 1911, Texas; *Pygmalion*, 1920, British Museum, Add. 50644.

[109] Rehearsal notes: *Man and Superman*, undated, British Museum, Add. 50732; *Arms and the Man*, 1919, Burgunder Collection.

[110] Rehearsal notes: *Man and Superman*, 1907, British Museum, Add. 50735; *Macbeth*, 1926, British Museum, Add. 50644.

responds, 'Well, is she? A woman I bring into my house is my guest. A woman you bring into my house is my guest. But a woman who drops bang down out of the sky into my greenhouse and smashes every pane of glass in it must take her chance.' Tarleton, said Shaw, should emphasize, 'A woman whom *you* bring into my house is my guest', and Summerhays should 'Acknowledge'. In *Pygmalion*, when Liza reclaims from Mrs Pearce the handkerchief Higgins gave her, exclaiming, 'He gev it to me, not to you,' Pickering laughingly agrees with Liza. Shaw told Liza, 'Give him an appreciative wink'.[111]

Sometimes his desire for realistic give and take between characters led him, during rehearsals, to add not only business but also exclamations and lines. In *Getting Married*, Lesbia says to the General, 'Have you no imagination? Do you think I have never been in love with wonderful men? heroes! archangels! princes! sages! even fascinating rascals! and had the strangest adventures with them? Do you know what it is to look at a mere real man after that?' A rehearsal note suggested that, on 'even fascinating rascals', the General should say 'Lesbia!' in a tone of 'remonstrance'. In the second act of *Pygmalion*, when Higgins tells Liza, 'If youre good and do whatever youre told, you shall sleep in a proper bedroom, and have lots to eat, and money to buy chocolates and take rides in taxis. If youre naughty and idle ...', rehearsal notes indicated Liza's response: on 'chocolates', her 'Mouth waters', and on 'taxis', she says, 'Aw *should* lawk to take a taxi.'[112] Even for *Macbeth*, Shaw provided verbal responses to help achieve a sense of interplay among the characters. When Ross tells Macduff, 'Your castle is surprised; your wife and babes / Savagely slaughter'd' (IV, iii, 204-5), Shaw noted in parentheses Malcolm's responses: 'Your castle is surprised (not) your wife & children savagely slaughtered (Oh)'.[113] The responses, of

111 Rehearsal notes: *Misalliance*, 1910, Hanley Collection; note in margin of Shaw's rehearsal copy of *Pygmalion*, p. 17, used for 1914 London production, British Museum, Add. 50639.
112 Rehearsal notes: *Getting Married*, 1908, Enthoven Collection; *Pygmalion*, 1920, British Museum, Add. 50644.
113 Rehearsal notes, *Macbeth*, 1926, British Museum, Add. 50644.

course, build to Malcolm's 'Merciful heaven!' which follows
Ross's speech. As a critic, Shaw delighted in ensemble acting.
As a director, he tried to produce ensemble playing. Helping
his actors motivate their actions and words, making them aware
of the tension between text and subtext, prompting them to
respond to other characters – occasionally with business, exclamations, or lines – assisting them in dissecting their speeches
into small and clearly differentiated units, Shaw tried to create a
moment-to-moment reality, an illusion that the events were
occurring for the first time, and a sense of realistic interplay
among characters.

MECHANICAL TECHNIQUE

Shaw's concern with the internal, motivational aspects of
acting did not lead him to neglect the external, mechanical aspects.
When a mechanical problem confronted him, he usually tried
to solve it by technical means – emphasis, tempo, or tone of voice,
for example – though sometimes he added explanations regarding
characterization, motivation, and the like. Of course, rehearsal
notes, written hurriedly in a dark theatre as actors go through an
entire scene or act without interruption, frequently use technical,
mechanical terms because it is more convenient for the director
to jot down 'slower' or 'angrily' than to compose an explanation
of why a passage should be delivered more slowly or why a
character is angry.

His letters to actors often combined explanatory statements
with technical instructions. In the examples used in the previous
section, the stress was on the former; here, the emphasis is on the
latter. After a rehearsal of *John Bull's Other Island*, Shaw wrote
to John L. Shine (Larry Doyle):

> In the last scene you say to Keegan 'In heaven, I suppose'.
> The exact words are 'Oh, in heaven, no doubt', which sounds
> more sceptical. . . . Then there is 'Yes, yes: I know that as
> well as you do'. The 'Yes, yes' gives a much better effect of
> nervous irritability than an improvised substitute. Today you

said 'undersell England in the EYES of the world' instead of 'markets of the world', which is bad political economy.[114]

Not only did he give the correct lines, but he analysed the differences in meaning between these lines and Shine's substitutions. On some occasions, he wrote such explanations during rehearsals – telling Higgins, for example, that he should not change 'I'm devilish sleepy' to 'Devilish tired', because 'He is never tired: he's sleepy'. Usually, Shaw's rehearsal notes on line readings are entirely technical: they give the incorrect version and the correct one. Rummy Mitchens (*Major Barbara*) should say, ' "at the other gate in Cripp's Lane", not "in the other lane at C's gate" '; Sir Patrick Cullen (*The Doctor's Dilemma*) should not change the verb in 'His brother-in-law extirpated tonsils for two hundred guineas' to 'exterminated' and the Inquisitor (*Saint Joan*) should say, 'vain and ignorant persons setting up their own judgments against the Church' instead of 'setting themselves up'.[115]

Shaw insisted on both the correct line and on what he considered to be the correct emphasis. Sometimes he gave reasons for this emphasis. Matt Haffigan asks, 'Fadher Dempsey: wouldnt you think well to ask him what he manes about the lan?' Larry Doyle answers, 'I'll tell you, Matt.' Shaw's rehearsal note gave both the emphasis and the explanation: ' "*I'll* tell you, Mat" – that is, *I*, not Father D.'[116] Post cards to Ellen Terry exaggeratedly explained emphasis in Lady Cicely's lines:

Have you ever thought of the GRANDEUR of wickedness?
Grand! Thats the word. Something grandly wicked. Not very wicked, not dreadfully wicked, not shocking wicked, but
GRANDLY WICKED.
GRANDIOSO

114 Letter to John L. Shine, Oct. 29, 1904, Hanley Collection.
115 Rehearsal notes: *Pygmalion*, 1914, Hanley Collection; *Major Barbara*, 1905, British Museum, Add. 50733; *The Doctor's Dilemma*, 1913, Texas; *Saint Joan* 1924, British Museum, Add. 50644.
116 Rehearsal notes, *John Bull's Other Island*, undated, Hanley Collection.

SOMETHING Grandly WICKED to their enemies.

and:

> *Thats what English people are like, Captain Kearney.*
> Yes, positively.
> *Thats* what English people are like.
> No use your contradicting it, Captain Kearney. I tell you
> THATS what English people are like.[117]

Usually, Shaw's rehearsal notes concerning emphasis indicated only the emphasis he wanted – as in various lines of Hypatia (*Misalliance*): 'Jerry would drive me MAD', 'Well, what *would* you call a man proposing to a girl who might be – ', 'They never *do* anything' – or else the desired and undesired emphasis, such as Undershaft's ' "The fourth had no *literary* turn", not "*had* no literary turn" ', Dubedat's ' "Do you mean *operate* on me" – not "operate on *me*" ', Baudricourt's ' "You think the girl can work *miracles*, do you?" not "the *girl* can work" &c.'[118]

Shaw was also meticulous about phrasing and pauses. According to Dame Sybil Thorndike, 'He disliked that awful habit of pausing after a conjunction, illogically ("I don't know why, but – I love you") rather than before it, logically ('I don't know why – but I love you")'.[119] On Doolittle's (*Pygmalion*) 'I cant carry the girl through the streets like a blooming monkey, can I?' Shaw indicated that there should be no pause before 'blooming monkey'. Summerhays, trying to prevent Hypatia from describing her experience in the woods with Percival – 'Please dont tell us this. It's not fit for old people to hear!' – should 'Mind the full stop' after the first sentence. When Bluntschli tells Raina, 'you recognize my uniform? Serb!' Shaw admonished the actor not to say the last two words like 'UniformSerb' but to 'divide them'.[120] Clearly, he used punctuation to indicate pauses.

[117] Postal cards to Ellen Terry, March 14, 1906, in *Terry-Shaw*, pp. 344-5.

[118] Rehearsal notes: *Misalliance*, 1910, Hanley Collection; *Major Barbara*, 1905, British Museum, Add. 50733; *The Doctor's Dilemma*, 1913, Texas; *Saint Joan*, 1924, British Museum, Add. 50644.

[119] Interview with Dame Sybil Thorndike, June 29, 1964.

[120] Rehearsal notes: *Pygmalion*, 1914, Hanley Collection; *Misalliance*, 1910, Hanley Collection; *Arms and the Man*, undated, Enthoven Collection.

Precise about movements as well as about lines, Shaw sometimes explained why the actor should or should not move on a particular line. He instructed Annie Russell, who played Major Barbara, that when Undershaft says,

'neither reason, nor morals, nor the lives of other men', turn away; but do not leave your place. I think it would be better not to move until, on the line 'It is no use running away from wicked people' you can emphasize your refusal to go with your mother by going right over to her chair, and standing behind it for a while. This avoids the risk of masking Lomax when he makes his speech. Afterwards, when he jumps up at the cue 'Mr Lomax is sitting on them', keep the line of sight open for him.

For the same reason, the Devil (*Man and Superman*) should 'get RC – . . . [and not] mask Ana' on his line, 'Don Juan: shall I be frank with you?' However, explanations do not usually accompany Shaw's mechanical blocking notes, which concern such matters as sitting and rising, or movement from one part of the stage to another. Ellie Dunn, for example, should not cross to stage centre, but should 'Keep RC' on 'But why did you do that, Hesione?' While planning these movements, Shaw kept motivation in mind. In his prompt-script for *Pygmalion*, he noted in the margin that Higgins 'Finally sits down on the piano bench to escape Doolittle's caresses'.[121]

One of Shaw's mechanical directorial responsibilities was checking sightlines. In the first act of *Arms and the Man*, he observed, '3d row of stalls cut off – ottoman too far up [stage]'. In *Misalliance*, Gunner pokes his head out of the Turkish bath, so the director must 'test visibility of head in Turkish bath from stalls'.[122] In blocking his plays, Shaw kept in mind, as most

121 Letter to Annie Russell, Nov. 27, 1905, Manuscript Room, New York Public Library; rehearsal notes: *Heartbreak House*, 1921, Burgunder Collection; *Man and Superman*, 1907, British Museum, Add. 50735; note in margin of Shaw's rehearsal copy of *Pygmalion*, p. 31, used for 1914 London production, British Museum, Add. 50639.
122 Rehearsal notes: *Arms and the Man*, 1919, Burgunder Collection; *Misalliance*, 1910, Hanley Collection.

directors do, the fact that all members of the audience should be able to see the action.

Shaw occasionally wrote reminders to himself and to the actors about the difficulties they would encounter in making adjustments from rehearsal conditions to performance conditions. Because movements in ancient Egyptian clothes differ from those in modern English clothes, Shaw indicated that some scenes of *Caesar and Cleopatra* required special rehearsal with costumes and slippers. Because the rehearsal area was smaller than the stage, he reminded Catherine (*Arms and the Man*), that in performance her walk to the electric bell would be longer.[123] Preparing a revival of *John Bull's Other Island*, he implored Barker to let the cast use the Court Theatre's stage and scenery, reminding him that on a previous occasion the scenery 'knocked [Louis] Calvert to pieces'.[124]

Directions concerning the actor's emotions or attitudes were often written not in motivational terms but in 'result terms' – that is, a statement of the feeling that the actor should convey, but not the cause of that feeling. Marchbanks was told that he should appear 'more lost' when he says, 'She said I'd understand; but I dont', and 'more imposing' when he says, 'Either the truth or a lie'. Tanner should be 'more joyous' on 'It's agreed that we all stand by Violet', but is 'not grave enough' on 'I trust, Enry, that, as between employer and engineer, I shall always know how to keep my proper distance, and not intrude my private affairs on you'.[125]

Shaw's notes frequently directed the actor in such mechanical techniques as where to look or how to deliver a line (as opposed to why). In the opening scene of *Major Barbara*, Stephen was instructed not to 'look as much at' Lady Britomart. Cusins was advised to 'lift' the passage beginning, 'Homer, speaking of Autolycus'. Shaw sometimes gave stage directions in terms of speed. Lady Britomart's speeches in the opening scene are

---

123 Rehearsal notes: *Caesar and Cleopatra*, 1912, Texas; *Arms and the Man*, 1911, Texas.
124 Letter to Granville Barker, March 14, 1906, in *Shaw-Barker*, p. 59.
125 Rehearsal notes: *Candida*, 1920, British Museum, Add. 50644; *Man and Superman*, 1907, British Museum, Add. 50735.

delivered 'too quick[ly] for an exposition', and she must 'Slow down the explanation about U[ndershaft]'s queer morals'. 'Tumble this out,' he told Marchbanks about one line; 'slow slow', he warned Candida about another.[126]

On some occasions, Shaw's instructions were in musical terms. One recalls his 'musical' interpretations of Shakespeare: his advice to Mrs. Patrick Campbell, for example, to consider Shakespeare's music rather than his characterization:

> . . . if you get the music right, the whole thing will come out right. And neither he nor any other musician ever wrote music without *fortissimi* and thundering ones too. . . . It is not by tootling to [Macbeth] *con sordino* that Lady Macbeth makes Macbeth say 'Bring forth men children only'. She lashes him into murder.
>
> And then you must modulate. Unless you can produce in speaking exactly the same effect that Mozart produces when he stops in C and then begins again in A flat, you cant play Shakespear.[127]

Shakespeare, according to Shaw, achieved his effects by 'word music' – that is, by doing with words, rhythms, rhymes, and the like, what Mozart does with music. Replace one of his poetic passages by a prose paraphrase and 'you have nothing left but a platitude that even an American professor of ethics would blush to offer to his disciples'. Speak the poetry unmusically, and the 'audience [will] wince as if [the actor] were singing Mozart out of tune'.[128]

Shaw discussed his own plays in musical terms: 'I . . . wrote long rhetorical speeches like operatic solos, regarding my plays as musical performances'. When Robert Loraine played Don Juan in *Man and Superman*, Shaw annotated his script like a symphony. 'The margin in the book,' said Winifred Loraine,

---

126 Rehearsal notes: *Major Barbara*, 1935, British Museum, Add. 50644; *Candida*, 1920, British Museum, Add. 50644.
127 Letter to Mrs Patrick Campbell, Jan. 13, 1921, in *Shaw-Campbell*, pp. 248-9.
128 *Our Theatres in the Nineties*, III, 76-7.

'twinkled with crotchets, crescendoes and minims; with G clefs, F clefs, and pianissimos . . .'.[129] According to G. W. Bishop, Shaw performed a similar service for Scott Sunderland when he acted Cain in *Back to Methuselah*. Cain's first long speech, in which he asks whose fault it was that he killed Abel, should be delivered, 'say, in C Major'. When he confesses that he envied Abel's happiness and freedom, Shaw asked him to 'drop without modulation to A flat, and abandon all affectation. He is now *talking about himself*, and much more serious than when he was talking about Abel.' When protesting that he does not want to kill women, he was to 'begin at a low pitch and drag the time a little; then take the whole speech as a *crescendo – p*. to *ff*'. Beside the words 'fighting, fighting, killing, killing' is the musical direction '*martellato*', and next to 'burning, overwhelming life', '*meno mosso*'. When he declares that he revolts against the clay, he should reach 'his top note; it is the climax – and indeed the end – of this part. His style in this speech is large and grand and harmonious, in longer bars, a little restrained in speed, but otherwise all out.' Bishop adds that Shaw was able to do this because the actor understood Mozart.[130] Dame Sybil Thorndike reports that Shaw treated his dialogue almost as a musical score. At times, he would even give the actor a musical tune for a line reading. 'He would say something like,

"No, no, not this: but this: ''

He worked to get the right *sound*.'[131] His rehearsal notes contain many examples of musical direction. When Ana asks, 'Has even death failed to refine your soul, Juan?' she should 'sing it like a dirge'. For the first London production of *Pygmalion*, Shaw freely used directions in musical terms for Beerbohm Tree and

129 *Shaw on Theatre*, p. 220; Loraine, *Head Wind*, p. 90.
130 Bishop, *Barry Jackson*, pp. 28-9.
131 Interview with Dame Sybil Thorndike, June 29, 1964.

Mrs. Patrick Campbell: 'The crescendo accelerando is softened away', 'Tenor register', 'Dont go back to *Tannhauser*', 'Andante tranquilo', 'f'.[132]

In a frequently quoted story of a conversation between Shaw and Arnold Daly,[133] the playwright tells the actor, 'All that it is necessary for you to do is to say my lines so slowly and clearly that the audience can hear every word.' 'What about my acting?' asks Daly. 'As long as they can hear my lines,' replies Shaw, 'you can act or not, as you please.' The story may be – and probably is – untrue, but the 'moral' is valid: speech was very important to Shaw. Emphasizing this aspect of Shaw's directing technique, Dame Sybil Thorndike declared that although 'he minded character, he paid more attention to the reading of the lines than to anything else. Speech was the main concern. One would get the thought through the language. The reality and the sincerity came from the voice and personality. His actors have to be good public speakers.'[134] Sir Lewis Casson agrees: 'To Shaw, careless speaking was as unpardonable as careless singing in opera – or careless dancing in ballet.'[135] The accuracy of these statements is evidenced by the importance which Shaw himself explicitly attached to good speech. 'Saturated with declamatory poetry and rhetoric from her cradle', he wrote admiringly of Lillah McCarthy, she learned the art of acting outside London 'by doing work in which you were either heroic or nothing'. In the fashionable London theatres, the 'art of acting rhetorical and poetical drama . . . became a lost art. . . . Rhetoric and poetry vanished with it. But when I dragged rhetoric and poetry back its executive technique became again indispensable.' Lillah McCarthy 'combined the executive art of the grand school with a natural impulse to murder the Victorian

132 Rehearsal notes: *Man and Superman*, 1907, British Museum, Add. 50735; *Pygmalion*, 1914, Hanley Collection.
133 For example, Langner, *G.B.S.*, p. 12; Hardwicke, *A Victorian in Orbit*, p. 155.
134 Interview with Dame Sybil Thorndike, June 29, 1964.
135 Sir Lewis Casson, 'A Remembrance', in *Setting the Stage: A Guidebook to Season '66: The Minnesota Theatre Company, Fourth Season* (Minneapolis: Tyrone Guthrie Theatre, 1966), p. 21.

womanly woman; and this being just what I needed I blessed the day when I found her . . . '.[136]

Even before he was a regular theatre critic, Shaw was adamant about good speech. 'I am alive to the necessity of perfect diction when an attempt is made at realism in the pitch of conversation,' he wrote William Archer in 1889, and then complained of Charles Charrington's production of *A Doll's House*: 'I was in the fourth row of the pit, which is not unreasonably far back; but I lost several lines, and was conscious of a great relief when [the actors] spoke out or made their words tell.'[137] As a theatre critic, he continually discussed voice and diction – reminding Lena Ashwell, for example, that 'there are short vowels in the dictionary as well as long vowels', that the first vowel in 'fascination' should not be so long as to necessitate the omission of the second; and praising Mabel Terry's ability to 'speak beautifully, without the slightest trick or mannerism of any sort . . .'.[138]

As a director, he worked for audibility and good diction. Such reproofs as 'not audible', 'indistinct', and 'quite inaudible' appear in rehearsal notes of every production he either directed or supervised. He frequently noted sloppy diction, warning Lady Macbeth, for instance, that 'milk of human kindness' (I, v, 18) sounded like 'milkahumankindness', that 'nature's mischief' (I, v, 51) sounded like 'naycher's mischief', that 'the owl that shriek'd' (II, ii, 3) sounded like 'Yowl that shrieked'.[139] Bad diction sometimes inspired him to compose extravagant lectures to the erring actor. When Cedric Hardwicke was playing Magnus in *The Apple Cart*, Shaw reprimanded him for having

tried the extraordinary experiment of delivering your big speech, and a great deal of the rest of the play, without a single article, definite or indefinite, a single preposition, a single conjunction; in short, without any grammatical structure

[136] *Shaw on Theatre*, pp. 222-5.
[137] Letter to William Archer, June 11, 1889, in *Collected Letters*, p. 214.
[138] *Our Theatres in the Nineties*, II, 40; III, 373.
[139] Rehearsal notes, *Macbeth*, 1926, British Museum, Add. 50644.

except an occasional interjection and a precarious supply of verbs. There was not a solitary *but* from one end to the other; yet 'but' is the most important conjunction in the English language. 'Be not faithless believing' may sound well; but it doesnt make sense, and bewilders where it should impress. . . . In the pantomime of Robinson Crusoe, which I saw as a boy, Man Friday delivered a stump speech; and whenever he said 'But', the goat went for him. If that goat had been on the stage on Monday you would have cut his part clean out. Any good Catholic will tell you how important first and last words are (see 'The Garden of Jesus' and other devotional works); but you always omit the firsts and drop the lasts. It is a tragic thing to see you wrecking a great career by despising words of less than three syllables, and shortening the three into two. . . . Take care of your buts and thoughs and fors and first syllables at the beginnings of the sentence and definite articles, and a great career is within your grasp. Neglect them, and your doom will be obscurity, poverty, ruin, despair, disgrace, and damnation.[140]

Shaw's rehearsal notes for his plays comprise a textbook of good and bad speech practices. Guard against dropping the end of a line, he told the actor: when Ramsden commands Octavius, 'dont call him Jack under my roof', Shaw noted, ' "roof" not heard'. Do not run words together, he warned: Hypatia's 'You may kiss me if you catch me' sounded like 'youskissmMatchy'. Do not add *r* to a vowel, he advised, as he told Bentley not to call Hypatia 'Hypasher'. Alert to the necessity of sounding initial vowels, he pointed out that Raina's 'After – after' sounded like 'after rafter'. Since words beginning in *h* create pronunciation problems similar to those in words beginning with vowels, he urged Captain Shotover to sound this letter: 'Dont swallow your articulation. "Now before *H*igh *h*eaven." ' He called for distinct articulation of consonants: Shotover should pronounce the word ' "Rum m m m m" not "ru*b*" '

140 Letter to Cedric Hardwicke, Aug. 20, 1929, in Hardwicke, *Let's Pretend*, pp. 205-6.

and Cusins' 'evangelical sects' must not sound like 'evangelical sex'.[141]

Shaw's preoccupation with diction led to a joke about mispronunciation in *Caesar and Cleopatra*. Caesar, unable to pronounce Ftatateeta's name, calls her 'Teetatota' or 'Totateeta'. Since Cleopatra and Ftatateeta herself must pronounce the name perfectly, Shaw indicated that they may learn to do so by practising it as 'Aftatateeta' and later drop the *A*. 'It will then be as easy as saying "left a message" or "laughed to scorn" or "lift a suitcase" or any other phrase with an ft in it'.[142] *Misalliance* contains a diction lesson: the Polish aviatrix, Lina Szczepanowska, teaches Tarleton how to pronounce her name.

LINA. Say fish.

TARLETON. Fish

LINA. Say church.

TARLETON. Church.

LINA. Say fish church.

TARLETON (*remonstrating*) But it's not good sense.

LINA (*inexorable*) Say fish church.

TARLETON. Fish church.

LINA. Again.

TARLETON. No, but – (*resigning himself*) fish church.

LINA. Now say Szczepanowska.

TARLETON. Szczepanowska. Got it, by Gad.

Since dialect is so important in *John Bull's Other Island*, Shaw composed for future directors of the play a set of instructions in which he warned that unless they exercise 'the most unsparing vigilance', the entire company would assume that 'mean is pronounced mane, sleep slape, &c by Irish people of all classes'. Although Larry Doyle 'must be an unmistakeable Irishman . . . his speech is that of a refined and educated man' and his pronunciation 'no better and no worse than the text indicates'.

---

[141] Rehearsal notes: *Man and Superman*, 1907, British Museum, Add. 50735; *Misalliance*, 1910, Hanley Collection; *Arms and the Man*, 1911, Texas; *Heartbreak House*, 1921, British Museum, Add. 50644; *Major Barbara*, 1929, British Museum, Add. 50644.

[142] Letter to Gabriel Pascal, no date given, in Deans, *Meeting at the Sphinx*, p. 41.

Although Father Keegan 'jocularly affects a brogue in his talk with the grasshopper and Patsy, [he] is a man of ascetic refinement and distinction, compared with whom an English Archbishop would seem only a respectable family butler'. Hodson should 'not drop his aitches except when he is excited – as indicated', nor should Aunt Judy 'mispronounce any worse than the text indicates'.[143]

Shaw's efforts to have the actors in productions which he did not superintend pronounce the dialogue precisely as the character would, took the extreme form, in *Major Barbara*, of writing out Bill Walker's cockney dialect quasi-phonetically, with traditional orthography. Thus, Bill says:

> Aw did wot Aw said Aw'd do. Aw spit in is eye. E looks ap at the skoy and sez, 'Ow that Aw should be fahnd worthy to be spit upon for the gospel's sike!' e sez; an Mog sez 'Glaory Allelloolier!'; an then e called me Braddher, an dahned me as if Aw was a kid and e was me mather worshin me a Setterda nawt. Aw ednt jast nao shaow wiv im at all. Arf the street pryed; an the tather arf larfed fit to split theirselves. (*To Barbara*) There! are you settisfawd nah?

– which, translated, is:

> I did what I said I'd do. I spit in his eye. He looks up at the sky and says, 'Oh that I should be found worthy to be spit upon for the gospel's sake!' he says; and Mog says 'Glory Halle-lujah!'; and then he called me Brother and downed me as if I was a kid and he was my mother washing me a Saturday night. I hadnt just no show with him at all. Half the street prayed; and the tother half laughed fit to split theirselves. (*To Barbara*) There! are you satisfied now?

In *Pygmalion*, written seven years later, he abandoned this practice shortly after the beginning of the first act: '*Here, with apologies, this desperate attempt to represent [Liza's] dialect without a phonetic alphabet must be abandoned as unintelligible outside*

143 'Instructions to the Producer [of *John Bull's Other Island*]'.

London.' Shaw's efforts to find a way to transcribe pronunciation with accuracy led him to set aside in his will a certain amount
of money for a new alphabet that would do the job. The result of
this provision is an edition of *Androcles and the Lion* with parallel
texts of the old and new alphabets.[144]

As an acting coach, Shaw's resources were astonishingly
varied. He drew on a wide range of techniques, motivational
and mechanical, 'internal' and 'external', to help the actor create the
the illusion of actuality. Concerned with the individual actor,
Shaw was at the same time aware of the ensemble. He aimed at
realism, but he also wanted theatrical effectiveness. Several aspects
of a director's dealings with actors – pace, building, and timing –
will be discussed in the next chapter, which deals more directly
with theatrical effectiveness.

---

[144] *The Shaw Alphabet Edition of Androcles and the Lion* (Harmondsworth: Penguin,
1962).

V

Stage Effects and Stage Effectiveness

Shaw arranged each stage picture so that it contributed to the impact of the play, but was also careful to see that the play did not become a mere pretext for lively scenic effects. This does not mean that he opposed scenic effects or stage machinery: he resisted them only when they threatened to become more important than the text. The play should not stop, he believed, in order for the scene technician to display his skill. When William Faversham was about to present *Misalliance* in the United States in 1917, Shaw warned him against overdoing the airplane crash. To create the illusion of the crash, Shaw insisted, all Faversham needed was a hamper filled with broken glass and actors who would look up and shout.[1] When Leon Schiller directed *Heartbreak House* in Poland in 1930, he wanted to introduce a Piscator-like motion picture at the end, showing two flying airplanes. Shaw opposed the idea, and he advised Floryan Sobieniowski, his Polish translator, to tell Schiller to write a programme note explaining that at the conclusion of the play 'there will be a cinema show by Mr S. whilst the audience is leaving the theatre'. Emphasizing that 'The aeroplanes are not dramatic characters in the play', Shaw urged Schiller to forget about an airplane film and instead 'devote himself to producing an illusion of their sound in the air. The best imitation is produced by a vacuum cleaner'.[2]

If special effects were essential to a theatrical effect, however, or if they enhanced the dramatic action, Shaw used them. Co-directing *Heartbreak House* in London, he carefully attended to sound-effects. When Mangan and Billy Dunn are blown up, he

[1] Letter to William Faversham, undated, Hanley Collection.
[2] Undated reply in margin of letter-questionnaire dated March 15, 1930, sent by Floryan Sobieniowski, Hanley Collection.

noted, 'Explosion no good.'[3] In *Arms and the Man*, Bluntschli's entrance is preceded by a burst of firing. Rather than have a series of rifle shots ad lib, Shaw timed the effect, calling for a fusillade of exactly five shots.[4] He even tried to get a believable sound-effect for the grasshopper in the second act of *John Bull's Other Island:*

> The grasshopper will not do in the provinces with that silly ginger beer bottle. We must go to Tisley & Spiller or some other maker of laboratory apparatus, and get one of the little whistles with which they test how shrill a note you can hear. Tiny brass things, with pneumatic blowers attached. We ought to have used one all through at the Court, but I did not think of the device until too late.[5]

When a stage effect did not overwhelm or get in the way of the play, but instead reinforced the dramatic point that the author intended, Shaw tried to make the most of it. To Forbes Robertson, he described in detail how he would stage the final scene of *Richard III*. Declaring that 'No actor has ever done the curious recovery by Richard of his old gaiety of heart in the excitement of the battle', which 'whirls him out of his vulgar ambition to be a king' and makes him once more an 'ecstatic prince of mischief', Shaw suggested how the actor playing Richard might realize the effects of this last scene:

> he should have a bucket of rosepink thrown in his face, and then reel on; all cut to pieces, killed already six times over, with a broken sword & his armor all in splinters, wrenching off the battered crown which is torturing his poor split head. Being hunted down just then by the Reverend Pecksniff Richmond & his choir, he is just able, after an impulse to hold on to the crown tooth & nail, to pitch it gaily to him & die like a gentleman.

Rosepink, splintered armour, and battered crown not-

3 Rehearsal notes, *Heartbreak House*, 1921, British Museum, Add. 50644.

4 Note in margin of prompt-copy of *Arms and the Man* (London: Constable, 1905). British Museum, Add. 50602. Although the date of the production is not indicated, the play was produced at the Savoy Theatre in 1907.

5 Letter to Granville Barker, July 20, 1907, in *Shaw-Barker*, pp. 96-7.

withstanding, Shaw's major emphasis – here as elsewhere – was on the actor, and in his staging of crucial scenes he tried to help the actor achieve the maximum effect. When Robert Loraine was playing the title role in *Cyrano de Bergerac*, Shaw suggested that he stage the final scene differently:

> I dont think Cyrano should fall. The whole point of the death is that he dies on his feet; and he ought to stiffen there and be visibly a dead man. To make this clear, Roxane, not realising that he is dead, should go to his assistance; and then the statue should fall, and fall stiff. To save your bones, one of the men, seeing what is happening, should catch him as he is falling away from her, and the two should let him down, still stiff as a poker at full length. Just try it in one or two ways. As it is, it is too obviously a stage fall; and the effect of the scene is so very fine that it is a pity to mar it by the slightest touch of artificiality.[6]

Not only was Shaw trying to help Loraine stage the scene more effectively, he was also aiming to nullify a stagey moment so artificial that the audience could not believe that a real thing was happening to a real person.

Shaw's own plays contain stage effects that imaginative directors can exploit. Music, dancing, and colourful masquerade costumes enliven the final act of *You Never Can Tell*. At the end of the second act of *Major Barbara*, a loud band blares forth a marching version of the Wedding Chorus from Donizetti's *Lucia di Lammermoor* as the heartbroken heroine repeats Christ's last words on the cross. The last scene of *The Devil's Disciple* has a melodramatic reprieve from the gallows at the eleventh hour. Scenery changes before our eyes in *Androcles and the Lion*, and an angel drops from the sky in *The Simpleton of the Unexpected Isles*.

However, Shaw was not content to let these effects 'play themselves'. An imaginative director himself, he took considerable care to enhance the effects written into the text. During the first

---

[6] Draft of letter to Forbes Robertson, Dec. 20, 1903, British Museum, Add. 50534; letter to Robert Loraine, April 19, 1919, in Loraine, *Head Wind*, pp. 260-1.

act of *Pygmalion*, the script calls for '*Torrents of heavy summer rain*'. His rehearsal notes request 'More horrible, finer rain! Cant we get the clouds to move & a moon to come out when the rain stops [later in the act]?'[7] Joan of Arc, entering the Court of the Inquisition in chains, creates a striking effect, but Shaw advised Joan on how to make it more forceful: 'When you come on in the trial scene, kick the chain from step to step instead of dragging it. Let the kicks be heard before you come in.'[8] Bluntschli's entrance from the balcony onto the pitch-black stage in the first act of *Arms and the Man* was made more vivid as Shaw the director, following through the implications in the text, asked for five rifle shots, and then told Bluntschli not to enter until their noise has died away.[9] For a split second, Bluntschli stands with the curtains apart, silhouetted against the dark blue sky,[10] following which he closes the curtains and pauses ominously before he speaks his first line in the dark: ' "Sh!" (dead silence) "Dont call out or youll be shot." '[11] Then, Raina lights a candle.

A former art critic, Shaw did not neglect the stage picture, though he derided compositional effects that sacrificed credibility, motion, and life to 'living pictures' with obviously posed models.[12] When Mrs Patrick Campbell was playing in Björnson's *Beyond Human Power*, he told her that George Titheradge's determination to die parallel to the footlights 'with his heels O.P. and his head P, whilst you occupy the corresponding position P & O.P. rather spoils the picture. After all, it is not natural that he should die unassisted . . . and it would be a great improvement if he would breathe his last in the arms of Horatio – say the sceptical parson who wants the miracle.'[13] By placing the actors in

7 Rehearsal notes, *Pygmalion*, 1914, Hanley Collection.
8 Copy of letter to Wendy Hiller, Aug. 17, 1936, courtesy Miss Hiller.
9 Rehearsal notes, *Arms and the Man*, 1911, Texas.
10 *Ibid.*, 1919, Burgunder Collection.
11 *Ibid.*, 1911, Texas.
12 For example, *Major Critical Essays*, p. 273; *Our Theatres in the Nineties*, I, 179-80.
13 Letter to Mrs Patrick Campbell, Nov. 7, 1901, in *Shaw-Campbell*, p. 7. In the English theatre, 'P' ('Prompt Side') is the side of the stage off which the prompter sits – usually, stage left. 'O.P.' is 'Opposite Prompt', stage right. Following the custom of the English theatre, these stage directions are from the viewpoint of the actor as he faces the audience.

positions suggested by the situation in the play, Shaw achieved both a more natural effect and a more interesting composition.

As a director, he tried to prevent awkward or pedestrian groupings. Seeing that Higgins, Liza, and Mrs Pearce were lined up in an evenly spaced row, which is a monotonous arrangement, he noted: 'Not XXX up at the door'. Later in the play, when he observed Doolittle, Pickering, and Mrs Higgins similarly lined up, he told Doolittle, 'get with Pick. ●● ● not ●●● '. With only two characters on stage, such as Raina and Bluntschli in the first act of *Arms and the Man,* he varied their relative positions so that they would 'open up' to three-quarter and one-quarter positions rather than face each other in profile throughout the scene.[14] But even though Shaw tried to avoid clumsy or dull groupings of actors, he eschewed beautiful compositions when they called attention to themselves as pictorial effects, for such effects distract from the situation in the play. When Joan of Arc assumes leadership of the army, he told Lawrence Langner, 'she should be in front of all the rest, in command of the stage in the good old-fashioned way from the point of view of the audience, and not beautifully composed in the middle of the picture with all the other people turning their backs to the spectators. Why dont you carry out my directions and get my effects instead of working for pictorial effects?'[15] His own plays indicate stage pictures that visualize important thematic content. Probably the most obvious illustration of this is the final curtain of *Candida,* when the poet rushes out, leaving the parson and his wife as part of a stage picture of bourgeois bliss: in a comfortable parlour, with the fire going in the fireplace, they embrace. This sort of cozy, domestic scene is uncongenial to the poetic temperament, and though audiences are not told this verbally, they are told it visually.

As a director, Shaw attempted at every opportunity to tell the story and convey the theme in a visual manner. When Robert Loraine, as Tanner, 'wanted to deliver the great speech about the

---

14 Rehearsal notes: *Pygmalion,* 1914, Hanley Collection; *Arms and the Man,* undated, Enthoven Collection.
15 Langner, *G.B.S.,* p. 75.

tyranny of mothers enthroned in the motor car, with Lillah [McCarthy as Ann] somewhere under the wheels with her back to the audience [,] I immediately saw the value of the idea, and put Lillah in the car in a fascinating attitude with her breast on the driving wheel, and Loraine ranting about on the gravel'.[16] Thus, the audience *sees* the windbag pontificating and the controlling woman seated womanly at – appropriately – the driver's wheel.

In trying to illuminate the play visually, Shaw frequently made use of stage business. When Tarleton sneaks back from an exhausting session at the gymnasium with Lina, Shaw asks him to feel his biceps as he enters. At a stroke, the audience remembers where he has been, sees the effects on him, and notices both a counterpoint and comic punctuation to the end of the previous scene: after young Hypatia dashes off in pursuit of Percival, enter old Tarleton, exhausted from his encounter with the object of his desires. In *Arms and the Man*, Bluntschli estimates Raina's age as '[not] much over seventeen'. She corrects him: 'Next time, I hope you will know the difference between a schoolgirl of seventeen and a woman of twenty-three.' Bluntschli is '*stupefied*' and exclaims, 'Twenty-three!' Raina then snatches the photograph from his hand, tears it up, and throws the pieces at him. At rehearsal, Shaw added stage business to help motivate the tear-up. He told Bluntschli to be 'more stupefied' when he exclaims her age, to '[look] at her, then at the photo to see if it is retouched'. *Then*, Raina snatches it and tears it up. The tear-up is made more effective by the rational Bluntschli examining evidence and thus further infuriating the already angry Raina. In *Pygmalion*, the director's additional business underscores the characters' desires and reactions. When Liza urges Pickering to buy a flower from her, Shaw suggests, 'Try to put the flower into his buttonhole.' The physical business points up Liza's sales technique and also Pickering's growing annoyance and ultimate surrender, as his response to the flower-girl alters from the apologetic 'I'm sorry. I havnt any change' (following which comes Liza's business with the flower) to the reprimand 'Now dont be troublesome: theres a

16 Letter to Granville Barker, May 24, 1907, in *Shaw-Barker*, p. 85.

good girl' and perusal of his pockets. Shaw's stage business aims to increase the naturalness of the characters' behaviour. When Higgins opens the second act with 'Well, I think thats the whole show', Shaw has him 'Pull a drawer out & recollect' before speaking. After the Porter has admitted Macduff and Lennox (*Macbeth*), Shaw suggests that he deliver the line, 'remember the Porter', which should prompt one of them to throw him a coin.[17]

Shaw, who admired stage business that illuminated the play, abhorred it as a substitute for what the playwright was trying to achieve. While admitting that Beerbohm Tree had 'some telling stroke' in each of his Shakespearean characterizations, he also pointed out that 'it is never one of Shakespear's strokes'. Tree's Caliban catches flies to stop them from teasing Stephano, his Richard II stifles a sob when his dog turns from him to lick Bolingbroke's hand, and his Benedick sits in a tree 'shying oranges at the three conspirators, and finally shaking the whole crop down on them when they accuse him of [being] "a contemptible spirit", quite content to exploit the phrase in its modern sense, though Shakespear means not contemptible, but contemptuous'. Some of these bits of business, Shaw conceded, were 'strokes of genius'; others, though, were 'inconsiderate tomfooleries (for you really should not, like Crummles's comic countryman, catch flies when another actor is trying to hold the audience); but they are all pure original Tree and not Shakespear'.[18] Shaw wanted stage business to bolster the playwright's work, not to compete with it.

Making certain that the action and plot are intelligible to the audience is part of the director's job. When Charles Charrington directed *A Doll's House*, the situation in the second act, Shaw wrote, was 'not made clear. The audience does not understand [Nora's] idea that Helmer will take the forgery on himself. When she exclaims "He will do it" they dont know what it means.'[19]

17 Rehearsal notes: *Misalliance*, 1910, Hanley Collection; *Arms and the Man*, 1922, Burgunder Collection; *Pygmalion*, 1914, Hanley Collection; *Macbeth*, 1926, British Museum, Add. 50644.

18 *Shaw on Theatre*, pp. 97-8.

19 Letter to William Archer, June 11, 1889, in *Collected Letters*, p. 214.

But when Charrington directed *The Wild Duck*, Shaw rejoiced that he clarified the situation and ideas.

> The same insight which enables Mr Charrington, in acting Relling, to point the moral of the play in half a dozen strokes, has also enabled him to order the whole representation in such a fashion that there is not a moment of bewilderment during the development of a dramatic action subtle enough in its motives to have left even highly trained and attentive readers of the play quite addled as to what it is all about.[20]

As a director, Shaw saw to it that important points 'carried' to the audience. When Gunner drew his pistol and examined it, Shaw directed him to turn in profile so that the audience could see what he was holding. At the beginning of the fifth act of *Caesar and Cleopatra*, Apollodorus appears on a stage crowded with extras, and calls, 'Hullo! May I pass?' Shaw warned him to pause after 'Hullo' until the audience has seen and recognized him, and only then ask whether he might pass. Otherwise, the audience would be confused as to who was speaking and why.[21] Since the intelligibility of dramatic action sometimes depends upon statements and motives that are made or revealed earlier in the play, Shaw was careful to emphasize the 'plants'. In the first act of *The Doctor's Dilemma*, Ridgeon asks Blenkinsop whether he can do anything for him; Blenkinsop replies, 'Well, if you have an old frock-coat to spare? you see what would be an old one for you would be a new one for me: so remember me the next time you turn out your wardrobe.' Blenkinsop, Shaw noted, must not speak confidentially but be 'Quite frank about the coat – Paddy must hear', for in the next act, when Walpole is about to take Blenkinsop home in his automobile, Sir Patrick asks Blenkinsop whether he has a sufficiently thick overcoat to wear in the motor-car. After Higgins tells his mother, 'Ive had to work at the girl every day for months to get her to her present pitch. Besides, she's useful. She knows where my things

[20] *Our Theatres in the Nineties*, III, 139-40.
[21] Rehearsal notes: *Misalliance*, 1910, Hanley Collection; *Caesar and Cleopatra*, 1912, Texas.

are, and remembers my appointments and so forth,' Shaw jotted down, ' "Besides, she's useful, finds all my things" – emphasize this.'[22] This passage, from the third act, needs emphasis because the audience must understand the reason for Higgins' despair in the fifth act: after his mother remarks that Liza has a right to leave him if she wishes, he complains, 'But I cant find anything. I dont know what appointments Ive got'.

Part of the directorial problem of making the action intelligible to the audience is focus: ensuring that the audience see what the director wants them to see, and guarding against distractions. Shaw tried to prevent actors from performing business or movements which would divert the audience's attention from the dramatic point being made by another actor. 'Dont fiddle about during BB's speech,' Shaw warned Dubedat. 'Dont get up until "Keep discipline" ', he told Raina; 'it takes attention off Bl[untschli]. Have a pause.' As director of the first London production of *Pygmalion*, he was constantly on the alert against scene-stealing by the two principals, Beerbohm Tree and Mrs Patrick Campbell. 'Dont destroy Doolittle with the business of the hat on the piano' while Doolittle is speaking, Shaw told Tree. And 'Dont spoil the exit of Mrs E[ynsford] H[ill]' by tomfooling with her coat. To Mrs Patrick Campbell he gave similar notes, asking her not to toy with her handkerchief while Pickering is talking, not to move on Tree's line, and not to talk through a speech by Doolittle.[23]

Pace, Shaw believed, is an essential preoccupation of the director: the play's rhythm must not falter because of movement, business, or failure to pick up cues. He advised the director:

Never have a moment of silence on the stage except as an intentional stage effect. The play must not stop while an actor

22 Rehearsal notes: *The Doctor's Dilemma*, 1913, Texas; *Pygmalion*, 1914, Hanley Collection.

23 Rehearsal notes: *The Doctor's Dilemma*, 1913, Texas; *Arms and the Man*, 1911, Texas; *Pygmalion*, 1914, Hanley Collection.

is sitting down or getting up, or walking off the stage. The last word of an exit speech must get the actor off the stage. He must sit on a word and rise on a word; if he has to make a movement, he must move as he speaks and not before or after; and the cues must be picked up as smartly as a ball is fielded in cricket. This is the secret of pace, and of holding an audience.[24]

Shaw's rehearsal notes reveal that he took his own advice. 'Take up this cue sharply,' Shaw told Soames (*Getting Married*). When Macbeth says, 'yet let that be, / Which the eye fears, when it is done, to see' (I, iv, 52-3), Shaw told him to start moving offstage on 'when it is done, to see', rather than after the line.[25]

Although the director may purposely break this 'rule', and all technical rules, in order to create a special effect, he must nevertheless be sparing in such special effects if they are to have any impact. Shaw recalled having seen 'a fine play of Masefield's prolonged by half an hour and almost ruined because the actors made their movements in silence between the speeches'.[26] His suggestions to Ellen Terry on playing Imogen contained advice on the subject of pace:

In playing Shakespear, play *to* the lines, *through* the lines, *on* the lines, but never between the lines. There simply isnt time for it. You would not stick five bars rest into a Beethoven symphony to pick up your drumsticks; and similarly you must not stop the Shakespear orchestra for business. Nothing short of a procession or a fight should make anything so extraordinary as a silence during a Shakespearean performance. All that cave business wants pulling together: from the line about ''tis some savage hold' to 'Such a foe! Good heavens!' you ought to get all the business of peeping and hesitating and so on packed into the duration of the speech, spoken without a single interval except a pause after the call. Otherwise it drags.

24 *Shaw on Theatre*, pp. 158-9.
25 Rehearsal notes: *Getting Married*, 1908, Enthoven Collection; *Macbeth*, 1926, British Museum, Add. 50644.
26 *Shaw on Theatre*, p. 159.

Mind, I dont propose that you should omit or slur anything, but only that you should do it with the utmost economy of time.[27]

The last sentence is crucial. Business should not be omitted or rushed through, but it should not hold up the dialogue. How this might be accomplished in his own plays is seen in the fifth act of *Pygmalion*, when Doolittle says, 'I, as one of the undeserving poor, have nothing between me and the pauper's uniform but this here blasted three thousand a year that shoves me into the middle class. (Excuse the expression, maam: youd use it yourself if you had my provocation.)'. Shaw's rehearsal notes directed Higgins to 'kick him' when he says what was then a minor obscenity, 'blasted'.[28] The realization of the meaning of that kick motivates Doolittle's parenthetical remark to Mrs Higgins, but the play does not stop for this business, since it is accomplished on the lines, not between them.

Although pace involves such practices as picking up cues and not stopping the dialogue for business, it is not merely a question of speed. When people complain that a scene is 'too slow', they mean that it bores them. The reason for the boredom, said Shaw, is not that the scene is paced too slowly, but that it is 'too fast to sink in' and therefore is 'empty of action & significance'. The remedy, most of the time, is not for the actors to go faster, but for them 'to go slower and bring out the meaning better by contrasts of tone and speed'.[29] Contrast gives the illusion of pace, for a particular scene will seem to be moving quickly when the scene that has preceded it is played in a slower tempo. Nor will the slower tempo necessarily seem to be too slow, for it will relieve the other scene. Variety of tempo helps achieve pace.

Shaw advocated many types of contrast. The play should be divided into smaller units, each with its own mood, tone, and tempo that contrast with the surrounding units. *Hamlet*, he said,

27 Letter to Ellen Terry, Sept. 23, 1896, in *Terry-Shaw*, p. 66.
28 Rehearsal notes, *Pygmalion*, 1920, British Museum, Add. 50644.
29 *Shaw on Theatre*, p. 158; letter to Elizabeth Robins, March 3, 1893, in *Collected Letters*, p. 385.

is a long play which can seem short 'only . . . when the high-mettled comedy with which it is interpenetrated from beginning to end leaps out with all the lightness and spring of its wonderful loftiness of temper'. In a review of *As You Like It*, he used a musical analogy, suggesting that the director divide the play 'into movements like those of a symphony. [He] will find that there are several sections which can be safely taken at a brisk *allegro*, and a few that may be taken *prestissimo*. . . .'[30]

As director, Shaw tried to provide contrast between individual scenes. In *Misalliance*, Summerhays' scene with Hypatia is followed by one between him and Tarleton. With Hypatia, the subject is sex; with Tarleton, parents and children. 'Make this speech brighter', Shaw told Summerhays about his first speech to Tarleton, 'to shake off the previous scene'. After an all-male scene in the second act of *The Doctor's Dilemma*, Jennifer enters. Shaw noted that her 'pride – gentle pride all through the part' should provide 'the relief after the men'.[31] He sometimes discussed scenic contrasts in musical terms. In the final act of *Man and Superman*, he told Lillah McCarthy,

> when Malone, Ramsden and Tanner go off making a great cackle and fuss, do not begin the scene with Tavy until the noise is over and the audience's attention has quite come back to you. Just wait, looking provocatively at Tavy, until there is a dead silence and expectation and then say, without the least hurry: 'Wont you go with them, Tavy?' Otherwise you will not get the new key and the slow movement.[32]

Each scene has its own 'key' and 'movement', which the director must find and have the actors play.

Vocal contrast is equally necessary. The actors' voices 'should not all have the same pitch nor gabble away at the same speed'.[33] The director 'must . . . take care that every speech contrasts as

---

30 *Our Theatres in the Nineties*, III, 271; *London Music*, p. 356.

31 Rehearsal notes: *Misalliance*, 1910, Hanley Collection; *The Doctor's Dilemma*, 1913, Texas.

32 Letter to Lillah McCarthy, June 7, 1905, in McCarthy, *Myself and My Friends*, p. 70.

33 Letter to B.B.C., May 27, 1941, Burgunder Collection. In this letter, Shaw notes that this principle is true for the stage as well as for radio.

strongly as possible in speed, tone, manner, and pitch with the one which provokes it', and should try to 'prevent the actors taking their tone and speed from one another, instead of from their own parts, and thus destroying the continual variety and contrast which are the soul of liveliness in comedy and truth in tragedy'.[34] During rehearsals, Shaw took many notes for this purpose. 'Dont catch [Joan's] speed as she comes in,' he told Dunois (*Saint Joan*); 'keep [your] curiosity about the stranger.' Keep 'cool against BB's fuss', he cautioned Dubedat. Reginald, about to describe Hotchkiss as a man with a face like a mushroom, should deliver his lines more slowly in order to contrast with the preceding speech by the General.[35]

Shaw also wanted each actor to achieve vocal variety. In Petkoff's long speech about the absurdity of washing every day, he noted, 'Speed not varied – all snapped out at the same rate.' When Ariadne compliments Hesione on her husband (*Heartbreak House*), Shaw pointed out that her speech should show 'extreme self-possession in contrast to excitement before'. For *Getting Married*, which is subtitled *A Disquisitory Play*, variety is essential in order to prevent the discourse from becoming monotonous. In Shaw's rehearsal notes, such entries as 'change of speed' appear frequently.[36]

Realizing that physical variety is as necessary as vocal variety, Shaw the director tried to vary the positions, business, and movements of actors. Higgins should move closer to Liza on the line, 'the streets will be strewn with the bodies of men shooting themselves for your sake before Ive done with you', for he should 'not always [keep] the same distance from [her]'. After the Russian Officer gives Raina a military bow, as the text indicates, he should 'Salute Catherine' (the text indicates that he bows to her as well). When Bluntschli interrupts Louka's scene with Sergius, in which she behaves independently, she should,

34 *Shaw on Theatre*, pp. 157, 282.

35 Rehearsal notes: *Saint Joan*, 1924, British Museum, Add. 50644; *The Doctor's Dilemma*, 1913, Texas; *Getting Married*, 1908, Enthoven Collection.

36 Rehearsal notes: *Arms and the Man*, 1911, Texas; *Heartbreak House*, 1921, British Museum, Add. 50644; *Getting Married*, 1908, Enthoven Collection.

129

'On entry of Bluntschli, get up at once, like a servant'.[37] The principle of contrasts was designed to 'hold an audience' by creating variety, and was in Shaw's mind from the process of casting through the final stage of rehearsals.

Pace and variety, while necessary to create and maintain theatrical excitement, are by themselves insufficient. Another essential element is building toward climaxes. As director, Shaw tried to prevent the action from proceeding on a single level. Within individual speeches, among groups of speeches, in scenes, and in the play as a whole, Shaw aimed – through increases and decreases in volume, tempo, intensity, and so forth – to create crescendos and diminuendos, climaxes and resting places. Small units within each speech received Shaw's attention. In the first act of *Major Barbara*, Lady Britomart tells Stephen of his father's defiance of conventional social and moral attitudes. Two-thirds of the way through the long speech, she says, 'I asked Gladstone to take it up. I asked The Times to take it up. I asked the Lord Chamberlain to take it up.' Although the climax occurs at the end of the speech, and the climax of that particular portion of dialogue occurs two speeches later, Shaw understands the necessity of a smaller build within the passage: his notes ask the actress to build in pitch from 'Gladstone' to 'Times' to 'Chamberlain'. Shaw did not, however, lose sight of the larger units. Whatever its components, a long speech has a climax which requires preparation. In *John Bull's Other Island*, Larry talks of giving tenant farmers a pound a week. When Father Dempsey replies that some of the landlords do not even make that much from the land, Larry retorts,

> Then let them make room for those who can. Is Ireland never to have a chance? First she was given to the rich; and now that they have gorged on her flesh, her bones are to be flung to the poor, that can do nothing but suck the marrow out of her. If we cant have men of honor own the land, lets have

37 Rehearsal notes: *Pygmalion*, 1914, Hanley Collection; *Arms and the Man*, 1911, Texas.

men of ability. If we cant have men of ability, let us at least
have men with capital. Anybody's better than Matt, who has
neither honor, nor ability, nor capital, nor anything but
mere brute labor and greed in him, Heaven help him!

Shaw warned Larry that 'If we cant have men of honor' should
'not [be] too high' since it is 'before a climax'. In the same way,
Shaw tried to create crescendos and climaxes in dialogue that
extended through several speeches. For example, there is an
exchange between Larry Doyle and Matt Haffigan:

MATTHEW (*sullenly*) What call have you to look down on
me? I suppose you think youre everybody because your
father was a land agent.
LARRY. What call have you to look down on Patsy Farrell?
I suppose you think youre everybody because you own a few
fields.
MATTHEW. Was Patsy Farrll ever ill used as I was ill used?
tell me dhat.
LARRY. He will be, if ever he gets into your power as you
were in the power of your old landlord. Do you think, because
youre poor and ignorant. . . .

Shaw's rehearsal notes for this dialogue call for:

Matt	What call have you	
&	What call have you	a row – crescendo.
Larry	Was Patsy Farrll	
	He will be	

Dubedat, arguing with the doctors for a full page, has a series of
speeches beginning, 'Oh bigamy! bigamy! bigamy!' and ending,
'Oh, go and do whatever the devil you please. Put me in prison.
Kill Jennifer with the disgrace of it all. And then, when youve
done all the mischief you can, go to church and feel good about
it.' Shaw called the actor's attention to the fact that he must not
reach his peak too soon, for the climax is in the last speech.[38]

---

[38] Rehearsal notes: *Major Barbara*, 1905, British Museum, Add. 50733; *John Bull's
Other Island*, undated, Hanley Collection; *The Doctor's Dilemma*, 1913, Texas.

The largest unit, of course, is the entire play. Shaw understood that the actor must marshal his energy and grade its expenditure from act to act. He must become more rather than less powerful in each succeeding scene, and prevent the audience from being bored by a sameness in his performance. In the title-role of *Captain Brassbound's Conversion*, Laurence Irving failed to build his performance in this manner. 'You are at present', Shaw wrote him,

> like a soldier who can do nothing but win the Victoria Cross, an astronomer who can do nothing but observe the transit of Venus, or the fabled American doctor who could not cure measles but was death on fits. You began the first act in the middle of the second, to the intense astonishment of the spectators. I am far from grudging Brassbound a certain sense of injury even in the first act; but you were a volcano smouldering with unutterable wrongs from your first step on the stage. When the right moment for the eruption came, the audience had acquired a Neapolitan indifference to lava, because there was such a lot of it about from the commencement that they became used to it.[39]

By failing to become more powerful, Irving did not succeed in remaining *as* powerful.

Pace and building are among the director's paramount concerns during the 'polishing' phase of rehearsal. Trying to increase the theatrical effectiveness of each scene, Shaw intensified his already scrupulous attention to detail, expending a great deal of attention on another aspect of polishing, 'timing'. On many occasions, he recorded that a character made an entrance too late, or too early. He had actors pick up their cues more sharply, or, on the other hand, more slowly – but the slow pick-up was timed for effect. For example, Lina's removal of her goggles, which reveals that she is a woman, prompts the other characters to respond verbally: 'Well I never!!!', 'Oh, I say!' and so forth. Shaw timed the effect, telling the cast, 'ALL. Count two of dead

---

[39] Letter to Laurence Irving, Dec. 26, 1900, Houghton Library, Harvard College.

silence when the goggles come off.' Movements, too, were precisely timed. In *Candida*, Prossy accuses Lexy of imitating Morell. A stage direction reads, '*coming at him*' as she says,

Why do you tuck your umbrella under your left arm instead of carrying it in your hand like anyone else? Why do you walk with your chin stuck out before you, hurrying along with that eager look in your eyes? you! who never get up before half past nine in the morning. Why do you say 'knoaledge' in church, though you always say 'knolledge' in private conversation?

As director, Shaw coordinated Prossy's '*coming at him*' to coincide with the repetitions of 'Why' in her speech, stopping after each movement to let the audience and Lexy take in what she says: 'Why – why – why – step step step & shove him to the sofa.' The rhythm of the movement reinforces that of the words and emphasizes the meaning of the speech. In *Arms and the Man*, Bluntschli's movement is timed with his speech. He tells Raina, 'My dear young lady, dont let this worry you,' and Shaw notes precisely, ' "My dear young lady" – cross – "dont let this worry" – sit – "you" '.[40] Since movement and speech are executed simultaneously, rather than alternately, the scene's rhythm does not falter or its pace flag.

Business and gestures were also coordinated with the lines. Cusins should not give Undershaft the trombone until he begins to speak the line, 'Blow, Machiavelli, blow'. Only on 'What the –' does Redpenny (*The Doctor's Dilemma*) throw down his pen. Dubedat is not to lift his hands until he starts speaking the artist's creed ('I believe in Michael Angelo . . .'). And in Lady Macbeth's sleepwalking scene, she puts her hands to her nose and makes a wry face on the line, 'Here's the smell of the blood still'.[41]

[40] Rehearsal notes: *Misalliance*, 1910, Hanley Collection; *Candida*, 1920, British Museum, Add. 50644; *Arms and the Man*, 1911, Texas.
[41] Rehearsal notes: *Major Barbara*, 1929, British Museum, Add. 50644; *The Doctor's Dilemma*, 1913, Texas; *Macbeth*, 1926, British Museum, Add. 50644.

Shaw was especially aware of the importance of timing in comedy. On several occasions, he warned actors to hold for laughs. In the fifth act of *Pygmalion*, he devised specific activities for the actors in case a laugh came during a speech, so that they would not be left simply standing on stage waiting for the laughter to die down in order to continue. In the middle of Doolittle's long speech about the good old days is the statement that some people once 'found a pram in the dust cart.' Telling Doolittle that he would 'probably [get] a laugh' on the line, Shaw directed Pickering to 'unclasp hands' when he heard the line, and told Higgins and Mrs Higgins to 'Play to "pram in the dust cart"'.[42] The reactions can adequately cover the duration of the laugh and keep the actors behaving in character. If there is no laugh, the responses need not delay the remainder of the speech.

But before the actor can hold for a laugh, he must first get it. To help him, Shaw used several devices, including pauses. When Undershaft, visiting his family for the first time in many years, is told by his wife, 'This is your family,' he replies, '(*surprised*). Is it so large?' During rehearsal, Shaw noted that his reply was 'too quick'. If Undershaft pauses before he speaks, perhaps looking at the five young people (including the fiancés of his two daughters) during that pause, the line would probably get a laugh. In *Arms and the Man*, Sergius tells Raina and Catherine the story of how Bluntschli escaped after the battle of Slivnitza, and concludes with the episode of the borrowed overcoat. A note told him to have 'More fun on the story'. Another note advised Raina, before speaking her next line, to 'Leave a pause for the story to fall dead flat'. When Tanner first enters in *Man and Superman*, he goes directly to Ramsden

> *as if with the fixed intention of shooting him on his own hearthrug. But what he pulls from his breast pocket is not a pistol, but a foolscap document* [Ann's father's will] *which he thrusts under the indignant nose of Ramsden as he exclaims*

> TANNER. Ramsden: do you know what this is?

---

42 Rehearsal notes, *Pygmalion*, 1920, British Museum, Add. 50644.

'Dont speak', Shaw told Tanner, 'until the will is under Ramsden's nose.' To point the laugh, Shaw also used the device of looking at someone before speaking. When Collins introduces Mrs George to Mrs Bridgenorth, Mrs Bridgenorth is directed to 'Look at Lesbia, [then] at Mrs George! – then – "Do you mean that Mrs G. is a real person" more abruptly'.[43]

For comic purposes, Shaw contrasted what is said and how it is said. In *Arms and the Man*, Catherine explains the use of an electric bell:

CATHERINE. You touch a button; something tinkles in the kitchen; and then Nicola comes up.
PETKOFF. Why not shout for him?
CATHERINE. Civilized people never shout for their servants.

In rehearsal, Shaw told Petkoff to 'howl' his question and Catherine to 'deafen' him with her reply. Here, the manner of delivery provides a comic comment on the words delivered, a subtext that contrasts with the surface text. For comic effect, Shaw also used the device of a sudden change in volume. In *Misalliance*, Summerhays reprimands his son, 'Bentley: you are not behaving well. You had better leave us until you have recovered yourself.' Shaw's rehearsal notes record the first word as 'Bentley!!!!' Then, 'With quiet severity', Summerhays delivers the remainder of the speech. Like father, like son. Immediately after Summerhays' instant change of volume, Shaw had Bentley use the same device. Bentley '*throws himself on the floor and begins to yell*'. Responding to this action, everyone starts talking at once. 'Leave him to me, Mrs Tarleton,' says Lina, who appears at the door. '(*Clear and authoritative*) Stand clear, please.' She lifts Bentley, throws him across her shoulders, and leaves with him, as Bentley says, '(*in scared, sobered, humble tones as he is borne off*). What are you doing? Let me down. Please, Miss Szczepanowska – (*they pass off out of hearing*).' Shaw told Bentley,

---

43 Rehearsal notes: *Major Barbara*, 1929, British Museum, Add. 50644; *Arms and the Man*, 1911, Texas; *Man and Superman*, 1907, British Museum, Add. 50735; *Getting Married*, 1908, Enthoven Collection.

'Keep yelling & stop suddenly with a change of tone for Lina.'[44]
The key word, which helps achieve the comic effect, is 'suddenly'.

Movement and gesture contrasting with the lines also increase
the comic potential of the dialogue. When Bill Walker declares
to Barbara that he is not afraid of Todger Fairmile – who is a
professional fighter and who outweighs him – Shaw asked him
to 'look outside' on the line. As Leo self-righteously labels as
'simple immorality' Lesbia's assertion that a woman should be
allowed to leave a man if she wants to, Shaw told her to 'put
her arm round Hotchkiss's shoulders' (Hotchkiss is the man for
whom she left her husband).[45] And he explained to Boanerges
that Magnus 'cannot get the effect on his "Shall we sit, ladies and
gentlemen" after B. sits down on [the previous line] "you might
as well call me Bo-Annerjeeze". You must make it by hastily
rising and sitting down again.'[46]

Shaw observed the actor as part of the total stage picture and
at the same time attended to minute details of execution. The
grouping of actors on stage, mechanical devices, stage business,
pace, contrast, building, timing – to enhance the theatrical
effectiveness of the scene and the play, Shaw used all of these. But
he employed these techniques as means of illuminating thematic
aspects of the play, not as substitutes for the effects intended by
the author.

[44] Rehearsal notes: *Arms and the Man*, 1911, Texas; *Misalliance*, 1910, Texas.

[45] Rehearsal notes: *Major Barbara*, 1935, British Museum, Add. 50644; *Getting Married*, 1908, Enthoven Collection.

[46] Letter to Matthew Boulton, Sept. 1, 1929, The Philbrick Library, Los Altos Hills, Calif.

VI

The Technical Elements
of Production

The prevalent view of Shaw's attitude toward the various technical or mechanical elements of production – such as scenery, lighting, and costumes – is summarized by Sir Lewis Casson: 'In his whole history as a producer of his own or anyone else's plays, I never knew Shaw [to] take any serious practical interest in anything beyond the casting and the acting. All the rest, including scenery, costumes, lighting and grouping, was of very minor importance, and personally, as a director, I sympathise with him.'[1] Apart from Sir Lewis' sympathy, the statement is simply not true. We have already witnessed Shaw's concern with the grouping of actors. As we shall see, he also took great interest in scenery, lighting, costume, make-up, and music.

SCENERY

As noted earlier, Shaw wanted the actor to make the audience believe that real things were happening to real people. In 1890, he implied a similar aim for the scene designer when he cited with approval the singer Victor Maurel's insistence that the scene designer produce 'an appropriate illusion as to the place and period assigned by the dramatist to the action of the piece . . . .'[2] Later, Shaw tended to modify this opinion, for he became more interested in the scenery creating the illusion of the world of the play, than in mere representationalism or pictorial realism.

When Shaw approached the scenic aspect of production, he combined his knowledge of art with his understanding of the drama. Condemning as an idiot the scene painter responsible

1 Mander and Mitchenson, *Theatrical Companion to Shaw*, p. 16.
2 *Music in London*, I, 97.

for the settings of *Cymbeline*, he told Ellen Terry that the scenic environment of her discovery of the headless man should be 'a land of lions [,] murderers and hobgoblins, with dreadful lonely distances and threatening darknesses. . . . I'd have painted such an endless valley of desolation for you that at your appearance in its awful solitudes, lost and encompassed by terrors, everyone would have caught [his] breath before you opened your mouth.' In *Hamlet*, he would 'make such a scene of "How all occasions do inform against me!" – Hamlet in his travelling furs on a heath like a polar desert, and Fortinbras and his men "going to their graves like beds" – as should never be forgotten'. Recognizing the importance of scenery, he advised Ellen Terry that if ever she played Shakespeare again, she should consider the scenery before she considered anything else, for 'art is one and indivisible' and the scenery is a vital part of the total picture.[3]

As a music and theatre critic, he was constantly aware of the scenery. He scorned such gross improbabilities as the mountains in the second act of *Die Walküre* 'being provided with flights of stairs and galleries exactly like the hall of an old manor house'. Abhorring scenic clichés, he reported that 'nobody could help laughing' at the collection of supernatural effects that Sir Augustus Harris assembled for *Der Freischütz*: 'illuminated steam clouds from Bayreuth, and fiery rain from the Lyceum *Faust*', plus the 'red fire, glowing hell-mouth caverns, apparitions, skeletons, vampire bats, explosions, conflagrations, besides the traditional wheels, the skulls, the owl, and the charmed circle'. Since one of the owl's eyes was larger than the other, it seemed to be looking at the audience through a monocle. 'To appeal to our extinct sense of the supernatural by means that outrage our heightened sense of the natural', Shaw concluded, 'is to court ridicule.' He objected when scenery called attention to its unreality – that is, when the scenic accessories were obviously false or inaccurate. In *Rosmersholm*, for example, 'the Conservative paper which attacked the Pastor for his conversion to Radicalism was none other than our own Globe; and the thrill

[3] Letters to Ellen Terry: Sept. 25, 1896, July 27, 1897, in *Terry-Shaw*, pp. 68-9, 193.

which passed through the house when Rebecca West contemptuously tore it across and flung it down, far exceeded that which Mrs Ebbsmith sends nightly through the Garrick audiences [when she hurls the Bible into the fire]'. Aware of the need to utilize stage space to produce an impression of largeness or smallness, he remarked that Forbes Robertson had not yet mastered the problem of disguising the spaciousness of the Lyceum stage when he had to show interiors. He deplored the shabby, makeshift scenery of a production of *John Gabriel Borkman*. In the first act, a hodgepodge of a Norwegian stove, a painted staircase, a few old chairs, and a 'faded, soiled, dusty wreck of some gay French salon' represented the Borkman home. The second-act gallery was not a gallery but an ugly, square box. In the third act, two back-cloths of a snowy pine forest and a mountain at midnight used the same set of wings and were placed upon an obviously wooden floor. 'When I looked at that', said Shaw, 'and thought of the eminence of the author and the greatness of his work, I felt ashamed.'[4]

The art critic's eyes saw ugliness and lack of harmony. Augustin Daly's textually mutilated production of *Two Gentlemen of Verona*, Shaw wrote, displayed a sense of colour that was 'cognate with Mr Daly's theory of how Shakespear should have written plays'. After diagnosing what was wrong with the scenery of *A Man About Town* ('an attempt at a harmony in two shades of terra-cotta, carried out in the wall-paper, curtains, and upholstery, is murdered by a ceiling, a carpet, and a conservatory, of such horribly discordant colors that it is difficult to look at them without a shriek of agony'), he suggested a remedy ('Why not repaint the ceiling, change the carpet, and fill the conservatory with a bank of flowers of the right color?').[5]

Illusion, beauty, and appropriateness are the triadic principles which underlie many of Shaw's statements on stage scenery. In 1895 he reviewed a biography of the comedian John Hare. That same year Adolphe Appia published *La Mise en scène du drame*

[4] *Music in London*, III, 249, 265-6; *Our Theatres in the Nineties*, I, 73; II, 66; III, 122-3.
[5] *Our Theatres in the Nineties*, I, 173; III, 10.

Wagnérien; five years later Gordon Craig designed Purcell's *Dido and Aeneas,* and not until ten years later did he publish *The Art of the Theatre.* Shaw's review of the Hare biography contains a plea for atmospheric and poetic scenery which is in harmony with these aspects of Appia's and Craig's ideas for scenic reform:

> It is one thing to banish vulgarity and monstrosity from the stage and replace them by conventional refinement and scrupulous verisimilitude. It is quite another to surround a real drama with its appropriate atmosphere, and provide a poetic background or an ironically prosaic setting for a tragic scene. There are some rooms in which no reasonable person could possibly commit suicide. . . .[6]

Gordon Craig's demands that scenery have beauty, simplicity, atmosphere, and suggestiveness fell in line with Shaw's ideas. As expected, Shaw consistently praised Craig's art, though, also as expected, he condemned Craig's unwillingness to grapple with the practical problems of theatre.[7]

Shaw's fondness for atmospheric beauty and his distaste for prosaic verisimilitude were partly reactions against exhibitions of Shakespeare that he witnessed. The nineteenth-century pictorial stage mangled Shakespeare's texts and framed what was left of them in two-dimensional scenery whose tawdry ugliness contrasted harshly with the poetic beauty of the dialogue. In 1895 Shaw complained that *All's Well That Ends Well* was 'pulled to pieces in order that some bad scenery, totally unconnected with Florence or Rousillon, might destroy all the illusion' which the language creates.

> Briefly, the whole play was vivisected, and the fragments mutilated, for the sake of accessories which were in every particular silly and ridiculous. If they were meant to heighten the illusion, they were worse than failures, since they rendered

6 *Ibid.,* I, 277.
7 See, for example, Shaw, *Pen Portraits and Reviews,* pp. 170–1; letter to Ellen Terry, undated, in *Terry-Shaw,* p. 342; *Shaw on Theatre,* pp. 174-6, 202-4, 206-12.

illusion almost impossible. If they were intended as illustrations of place and period, they were ignorant impostures. I have seen poetic plays performed without costumes before a pair of curtains by ladies and gentlemen in evening dress with twenty times the effect. . . .

On July 13 of that year, in a review of *A Midsummer Night's Dream*, he condemned Augustin Daly's failure to realize that his scene painter could not possibly compete with Shakespeare's verbal descriptions, and called Daly's ' "panoramic illusion of the passage of Theseus's barge to Athens" . . . more absurd than anything that occurs in the tragedy of Pyramus and Thisbe in the last act'.[8] A week later he reviewed the Elizabethan Stage Society's production of *Twelfth Night* on a platform stage. This method of staging, in sharp contrast with Daly's method, led Shaw to conclude, 'I do not, like the E.S.S., affirm it as a principle that Shakespear's plays should be accorded the build of stage for which he designed them. I simply affirm it as a fact, personally observable by myself, that the modern pictorial stage is not so favorable to Shakespearean acting and stage illusion as the platform stage.' Recalling a production of Browning's *Luria* ('acted – not merely read – in a lecture theatre at University College, against a background of plain curtains, by performers in evening dress'), he described its scenic effect as 'so satisfactory in comparison to the ordinary pictorial stage effect that I have ever since regarded the return to the old conditions of stage representation for old plays as perfectly practical and advisable'. A year later, when William Poel directed Marlowe's *Doctor Faustus* for the Elizabethan Stage Society, Shaw was even more enthusiastic:

> The more I see of these performances by the Elizabethan Stage Society, the more I am convinced that their method of presenting an Elizabethan play is not only the right method for that particular sort of play but that any play performed on a platform amidst the audience gets closer home to its hearers than

[8] *Our Theatres in the Nineties*, I, 28-9, 179.

when it is presented as a picture framed by a proscenium. Also, that we are less conscious of the artificiality of the stage when a few well-understood conventions, adroitly handled, are substituted for attempts at an impossible scenic verisimilitude. All the old-fashioned tale-of-adventure plays, with their frequent changes of scene, and all the new problem plays, with their intense intimacies, should be done this way.

In a review of Poel's 1897 production of *The Tempest*, Shaw praised his technique of creating illusion without illusionistic scenery. When Poel frankly told his audience, ' "See that singers' gallery up there! Well, lets pretend that it's the ship"', the audience agreed, willingly using its imagination to transform the gallery into a ship. 'But how could we agree to such a pretence with a stage ship? Before it we should say, "Take that thing away; if our imagination is to create a ship, it must not be contradicted by something that apes a ship so vilely as to fill us with denial of its imposture." ' Similarly, a superstitious person will see a ghost in a ray of moonlight on an old coat hanging on the wall, but will not be deceived by an elaborate, picturesque ghost. 'The reason is, not that a man can *always* imagine things more vividly than art can present them to him, but that it takes an altogether extraordinary degree of art to compete with the pictures which the imagination makes when it is stimulated by such forces as . . . the poetry of Shakespear.'[9]

However, Shaw pointed out, what is true for Shakespeare is not necessarily true for every playwright. A director who stages a modern realistic drama in verisimilar prose dialogue and asks us to imagine that the singer's gallery is a locale that is familiar to us, would be refused, said Shaw, modifying somewhat his suggestion that 'all the new problem plays' be staged in the Poel manner. It requires precise judgment, Shaw realized upon reflection, to know just how much help the imagination requires. Not only is there no general rule, but there is no general rule for any particular playwright. Bare-stage productions of *The*

9 *Ibid.*, I, 189; II, 184; III, 241-2.

Tempest and *A Midsummer Night's Dream* are better than
productions with the best scenery, which only destroys the
illusion that the poetry creates; but it does not follow that
scenery will not improve *Othello*. Shaw concluded that 'the
manager who stages every play in the same way is a bad manager,
even when he is an adept at his own way'. Shaw's eclecticism in
regard to stage scenery is typically linked to practicality: 'The
wise playwright, when he cannot get absolute reality of presentation, goes to the other extreme, and aims at atmosphere and
suggestion of mood rather than at direct simulative illusion.'[10]

Practicality informs Shaw's scenic techniques. In the review of
John Hare, Comedian, in which Shaw said that a drama should
be surrounded with an appropriate atmosphere, he makes an
equally revealing point about his relationship to the scenic conventions of the theatre of his day: 'I do not say that the stage
drawing rooms of the old Court and the St James's were better
than "four boards and a passion"; but they were worlds above
flats, wings, sky borders and no passion, which was the practical
alternative.' He always considered the practical alternative, and
in 1926 frankly admitted,

> I am tied down to what can actually be done with the theatre
> as it stands, and if you were to perform my plays in any sort
> of theatre but the one they were written for, you may have
> to mutilate them more or less horribly to make them prac-
> ticable. . . . [For] another sort of theatre I can write another
> sort of play, quite as good and fresher in form than the old
> one, but impossible of performance in the old nineteenth
> century theatres.

He praised Ibsen for asking – in *When We Dead Awaken* – that
the scenic possibilities of the theatre expand themselves to his
requirements, instead of the other way around, which was
Ibsen's custom. Shaw himself was no such innovator. He adapted
his own scenic requirements to the theatre of his time, but he was
quick to seize upon the scenic innovations of others – even, at

10 *Ibid.*, III, 243; *Androcles and the Lion*, p. 163.

one point, suggesting that Granville Barker play Hamlet, with Gordon Craig reproducing the scenery he had designed for the Moscow Art Theatre production, and possibly playing the ghost of Hamlet's father as well.[11]

The stage directions in Shaw's plays are notable for their detail. However, not all of the detail describes what the audience sees on stage. The three pages of stage directions that introduce *Candida*, for instance, tell about the appearance of the neighbourhood as well as the room on stage. While more than four pages of stage directions introduce *The Man of Destiny*, only seven lines describe the room we see. The rest concern mainly the history of Napoleon and the impact of a French army of occupation on an Italian village. *Widowers' Houses* and *Mrs Warren's Profession*, dealing with slum landlordism and prostitution, respectively, fit the category of 'social problem play' more closely than his other plays, and the scenic descriptions are unexpectedly sparse. Shaw describes the seven different settings of these two plays with little more than instructions for the relative placement of furniture and properties – in short, ground plans. Can this be reconciled with his detailed description of scenery in other plays: the very books in Morell's library in *Candida*, or the busts, portrait, and photographs in Roebuck Ramsden's study in *Man and Superman*? I think so. Shaw rightly considered himself 'A Dramatic Realist'.[12] As a realist he was concerned with the influence of social environment upon his characters, and the influence of his characters upon their social environment. When the characters' homes could establish a milieu and reveal an environment, Shaw used them for that purpose. The settings for the first two acts of *The Devil's Disciple* – the homes of Mrs Dudgeon and Mrs Anderson – contain the same scenic elements, yet their different arrangements reveal the distinct characters of these women. Since the social questions that are the subjects of *Widowers' Houses* and *Mrs Warren's Profession* concern environ-

---

11 *Our Theatres in the Nineties*, I, 277; *Shaw on Theatre*, pp. 182-3; Shaw, *Major Critical Essays*, pp. 109-10; letter to Granville Barker, Feb. 13, 1912, in *Shaw-Barker*, p. 180.
12 *Shaw on Theatre*, p. 18.

igures 1–5. Sketches, plans and instructions (by Shaw) for the French production of *The Devil's Disciple*, on five cards (in the Hanley Collection, Academic Center Library, University of Texas). Except for French titles (Figs. 1 and 3) and 'buanderie' (Fig. 1), the writing is in Shaw's hand.

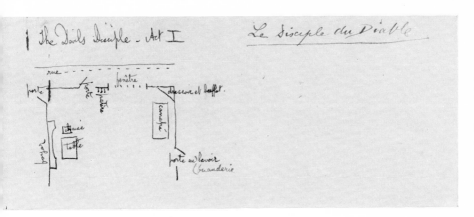

Figure 1. Ground plan of Act I.

On stage right is a 'fireplace', to the left of which are a 'table' and 'chair'. Upstage right is the 'door.' Upstage centre is another 'door' (leading outside), a 'rack' for hats and coats, and a 'window', beyond which is the street'. Upstage left contains a 'sideboard and cupboard'. Further downstage is a 'sofa', and below the sofa a oor to the scullery (laundry room)'.

Figure 2. Perspective sketch of Act I.

Figures 1–5. *The Devil's Disciple.*

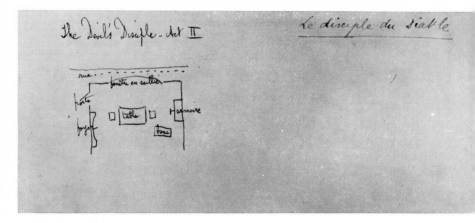

Figure 3. Ground plan of Act II.

On stage right is a 'fireplace', upstage of which is a 'door'. The upstage wall contains a 'bay window', through which we see the 'street'. Stage centre contains a 'table', downstage left of which is a 'settle'. stage right has a 'wardrobe'.

Figure 4. Perspective sketch of Act II.

On stage right is a 'fireplace', upstage is a 'bay window', and on stage left a 'wardrobe with Anderson's black coat hanging on the peg'.

ments that lie offstage, Shaw did not pay great attention to the scenic environment that the audience sees.

When the environment is abstract, as in the dream of Hell in *Man and Superman*, Shaw described no scenery at all. We see '*a man in the void . . . seated, absurdly enough, on nothing*'.[13] Significantly, when the Hell scene was produced under Shaw's supervision in 1907, the scenery aimed to simulate the void indicated in his stage direction: it consisted of stools covered with black velvet and draperies of the same material.[14]

Shaw's realistic framework contains elements of symbolism. *Arms and the Man*, for example, deals with the shedding of romantic idealism and the acquisition of a realistic point of view. The first act shows religious icons and other paraphernalia of romantic idealism in an aura of romantic moonlight. The second act, by contrast, presents newly cleaned linen drying in the sun. The third act takes place in an unromantic library; properties utilized in the opening action are papers and a pen, to compose businesslike, prosaic, military orders.

A symbolic progression also occurs in *Major Barbara*, in which Barbara and Cusins shed their illusions and acquire a realistic point of view. The first act takes place in Lady Britomart's home in fashionable Wilton Crescent – an actual London street, whose stately town houses reflect the unostentatious luxury to which the Stevanages are accustomed. In this environment, characters enjoy the benefits of romantic idealism. The second act takes place in the Salvation Army shelter in West Ham, a slum neighbourhood. Here, characters suffer from the economic and political inequities which allow the characters in the first act to enjoy themselves. The third act moves to a new location, the factory town of Perivale St Andrews. It is a place where work can be done; Undershaft offers Cusins a job, and Barbara sees that this is where she must work. Clean, efficient, without frills, the

---

[13] If an objection be raised that since the act was written with no thought of performance, this scenic description should not be taken into account, it could be answered that the author could then write *precisely* the type of scenic description he wanted, for he was not constrained to limit himself to the exigencies of the theatre as he knew it.

[14] McCarthy, *Myself and My Friends*, p. 108.

K

scenery features formidable instruments of power: a cannon, a shell, and an explosives shed. In this setting, Barbara and Cusins embrace Undershaft's offer of 'reality and . . . power'. These three scenes, moreover, embody – respectively – Don Juan's descriptions of hell, earth, and heaven in the third act of *Man and Superman*. He calls hell 'the home of the unreal and of the seekers for happiness', earth 'the home of the slaves of reality', and Heaven 'the home of the masters of reality'. The inhabitants of hell are insulated against social and political problems. 'Here you call your appearance beauty, your emotions love, your sentiments heroism, your aspirations virtue, just as you did on earth; but here there are no hard facts to contradict you. . . .' Earth is a place 'in which men and women play at being heroes and heroines, saints and sinners; but they are dragged down from their fool's paradise by their bodies: hunger and cold and thirst, age and decay and disease, death above all, makes them slaves of reality. . . '. In heaven, 'you live and work instead of playing and pretending. You face things as they are; you escape nothing but glamor; and your steadfastness and your peril are your glory. If the play still goes on here and on earth, and all the world is a stage, Heaven is at least behind the scenes.'[15]

During the second decade of this century, Shaw was still writing realistic plays, but he also began to write fantasies – a practice which he continued with greater frequency during the next three decades. Shaw's scenic descriptions show an increasing tendency toward simplification and suggestiveness, although he never completely abandoned realism in scenery, or in playwriting While the décor in the prologue to *Androcles and the Lion* is described simply as '*A jungle path*', other plays have considerably more detail. If it is important for us to understand the environment of the character who lives in the house, Shaw provides realistic scenic descriptions: for example, Captain Shotover's boat-like home in *Heartbreak House* is described in detail;

---

15 I am grateful to Professor Sidney P. Albert, of California State College at Los Angeles, for having called my attention to the relevance of the *Man and Superman* passage to the different settings of *Major Barbara*.

Higgins' laboratory and Mrs Higgins' drawing-room in *Pygmalion* have detailed, contrasting milieus, which provide appropriate visual backgrounds for the characters.

Other plays, however, employ suggestive, simplified scenery. Shaw cited with approval William Morris' contention that 'no more was necessary for stage illusion than some distinct conventional symbol, such as a halo for a saint, a crook for a bishop, or, if you liked, a cloak and dagger for the villain, and a red wig for the comedian'. In *Saint Joan*, Shaw created a fifteenth-century milieu through scenery as well as dialogue, but he did so by suggestion rather than by naturalistic means. The first scene uses '*a plain, strong, oak table*', with chair and stool, a '*mullioned thirteenth-century window*' with a wooden chest beneath it, to suggest the castle at Vaucouleurs. The second scene begins in front of a curtain, which Shaw does not describe. When the curtain is opened, two chairs of state on a dais, a curtained arch behind the dais, and a door suggest the throne-room in the castle at Chinon. The third and fourth scenes have still less description: a pennon in the wind suggests '*a patch of ground on the south bank of the silver Loire*', and a table and leather stools indicate '*A tent in the English camp*'. In the fifth scene, Shaw uses what he later referred to as 'a single pillar of the Gordon Craig type'[16] to evoke the ambulatory in Rheims Cathedral. In the trial scene, a row of arches stands for the '*great stone hall in the castle*', and the Epilogue uses one property to suggest Charles' bedchamber: a canopied bed on a dais. In each of these scenes, one or a few scenic elements symbolize an environment of which they are a part. Shaw's practice in *Saint Joan* harmonizes with the precepts of simplified, suggestive scenery enunciated by the theorists of 'the New Stagecraft'. His practice in *The Millionairess*, on the other hand, contrasts sharply with these precepts: Sagamore's office and The Pig & Whistle Inn are described in realistic detail. The practices in both plays, however, are consistent with the precept Shaw gave in his review of *The Tempest*: that one should

16 *Our Theatres in the Nineties*, II, 212-3; letter to Lawrence Langner, no date given, in Langner, *G.B.S.*, p. 58.

not stage every play in the same way. Although he used simplified scenery more frequently in his later plays, he varied his practice with the requirements of the individual work.

When Shaw directed his own plays, or was at hand when they were produced, he closely supervised their scenic preparations. He drew sketches and plans of the opening act of *Pygmalion*, with detailed instructions. For the 1906 revival of *Captain Brassbound's Conversion*, he sent J. E. Vedrenne photographs to be used as models by the scene painter. One photograph, he instructed, 'would do for the missionary's house in Act I. Of course it is a mosque, and impossible for such a purpose; but it is very Moorish; and nobody would know, especially if the decorations were planed off.' Another had 'the sort of divan seat that is wanted for Act II' as well as 'a simple & characteristic design for the tiling, and a good sample of a floor'. A third photograph 'gives the Koran inscriptions pretty plainly and a very good decorative arch. The window compartments also shew what the smaller door in Act II would be like.'

He had sufficient objectivity, however, to recognize when the results were bad. The scenery for the 1912 revival of *John Bull's Other Island*, which he supervised, turned out to be a 'grotesque . . . orgie of red lengths and pink lines and impossible rostrums covered with obvious old yacht sails died scarlet, such penny theatre wings, were never seen in any theatre'. After saying that the sky was 'beyond all description', he described it: the scene painter, 'stimulated to insane excesses by me, first covered it with flaming vermilion clouds. When he realized that they wouldnt move as at Bayreuth and that the sky had to do for Acts III and IV he tried to paint the clouds out, and now they look like claret stains.'[17]

During rehearsals, Shaw took notes on scenery and properties. He reminded the property master that Ramsden's copy of *The Revolutionist's Handbook* should be new; that Ridgeon (*The*

17 Sketch and working drawing of *Pygmalion*, Act I, Hanley Collection; letters: to J. E. Vedrenne, Jan. 10, 1906, Enthoven Collection; to Granville Barker, Dec. 25, 1912, in *Shaw-Barker*, p. 185.

Doctor's Dilemma), whose discovery is based on an actual discovery of Sir Almwroth Wright, should have for stage use 'a real pamphlet from Wright'; that the dummy soldiers which Undershaft kicks aside 'must be left more obviously in U's way' and that the shell upon which Sarah sits should have a red band; that in *Fanny's First Play* the piano-stool was filthy, the piano needed polishing, and the carpet was too small.[18] As a director, he wanted scenery and properties to be credible, to be appropriate to the character and to the practical needs of the dramatic action, and to have beauty.

When he was not at hand for productions of his own plays, he still tried to supervise the scenery. For the French production of *The Devil's Disciple*, he sent Augustin and Henriette Hamon, his French translators, floor plans and sketches of the scenery, with accompanying instructions in French, explaining how to accomplish quick scene shifts (see Figures 1–5). He also drew (probably on another occasion) a detailed sketch of the fireplace used in Acts I and II, with instructions in English. When the Berlin premiere of *Caesar and Cleopatra* was planned, Shaw wrote to Trebitsch,

> Will you find out for me *at once* what the mechanical resources of the Neues Theater are. All I want to know is, 1 Have they an electric turntable? 2 Have they hydraulic bridges? 3 Have they hydraulic clutches – that is, ropes to draw up weights from above – or is everything pushed up by a piston from below? 4 What is the depth of the stage from the footlights to the back wall and what is its width from side to side? Promise them drawings. I cannot draw; but I can make the painters and carpenters understand what I mean.[19]

Since the first act of *Caesar and Cleopatra* has scene-shifting problems similar to those of the last act of *The Devil's Disciple*,

18 Rehearsal notes: *Man and Superman*, 1907, British Museum, Add. 50735; *The Doctor's Dilemma*, 1913, Texas; *Major Barbara*, 1929, British Museum, Add. 50644; *Fanny's First Play*, 1915, British Museum, Add. 50644.
19 Sketch of fireplace for *The Devil's Disciple*, Acts I and II, Hanley Collection; letter to Siegfried Trebitsch, Aug. 10, 1903, Berg Collection.

Shaw composed a set of practical instructions for future productions of the play:

> In this act the scenes must be planned so as to enable the changes to be made without any interval, or at most very brief ones with tableau-curtains and continuous music. The sphinx and pyramid, with a back cloth representing the desert, can be ready behind the first scene. In the third, the desert cloth can be taken up; the wall of the square bay in which the throne stands can be shifted on in front of the Sphinx; the pyramid can be shifted off and the pillar wings on; and the throne and its platform, which should move on castors, can be pushed on. In this way the changes will be found quite practicable on old fashioned stages, where nothing but hand labor is available, and the Sphinx cannot be shifted.
>
> When hydraulic or electric machinery is available, the scenery can be improved accordingly; but the stage business should not be altered in such a way to make the dialogue ineffective.

In a similar set of instructions for future directors of *John Bull's Other Island*, he explained that the same back-cloth could be used for the three scenes of Acts II and III, and the same raked piece (the hill) for both scenes in Act II, but 'in the second scene the stone must be removed, the round tower pushed [on] as a wing, and the scene disguised by the change in the lighting'. Since scene changes '*must not occupy more than one minute at the very outside*', the first scene of Act IV must be shallow and the second scene set behind it. He also warned the scene designer that an Irish round tower does not resemble a ruined medieval castle and that an Irish land agent's house is not a thatched hovel.[20]

When he was in personal communication with the director or the designer, he sent pictures and wrote comments on the scenery. To William Faversham, who directed the United States

20 'Notes to Act I [of *Caesar and Cleopatra*]', undated typed manuscript, Berg Collection; 'Instructions to the Producer [of *John Bull's Other Island*]', British Museum, Add. 50615.

premiere of *Getting Married* in 1916, Shaw sent photographs of the original production, commenting that he himself had designed the scenery. When Faversham directed the United States premiere of *Misalliance* the following year, Shaw had no photographs of the original production. He therefore drew and sent a ground plan and perspective sketch.[21] (See Figures 6 and 7.)

Like his blocking instructions, Shaw's scenic instructions were detailed, but they did leave room for the designer's creativity. Although he gave scene designer Lee Simonson minute instructions on Captain Shotover's home, including a sketch, he also pointed out,

> So long as you do not alter or mask the positions of my people on the stage, or cut out an essential effect like the cutting off of the light and leaving the group in the dark, you may do your own job in your own way. The more of your own you put in, the richer the play will be . . . let yourself rip. Artist and author are co-equal and co-eternal – see the Athanasian creed.

Simonson complimented the scenic instructions in Shaw's stage directions for this play. The entrances, exits, and furniture, he said,

> are perfectly placed for the playing of the entire first act. The movements and the grouping of the actors take place easily, naturally, almost inevitably, as I realized when the play was put into rehearsal. The two window seats specified seem mere interior decoration until the second act, when for the scene with the burglar the cast of ten fills the stage. The window seat with its nautical lockers below takes the place of all the additional chairs or a couch that would otherwise have to be lugged on for this single scene or clutter up the stage and get in the actors' way for the rest of the time.

Shaw, Simonson continued, had 'made the setting, with its galleon windows and its nautical beaming – an enlarged captain's cabin –

21 Letters to William Faversham: Aug. 3, 1916, and undated, Hanley Collection.

a symbol of the meaning of the play, which is itself a symbol of the fate of a floundering ship of state. This is exactly what an imaginative designer should have done if the stage directions had been nothing more than "Captain Shotover's study in his Sussex county home".[22]

LIGHTING

'If I had never been taught to use my eyes as a critic of pictures,' Shaw wrote in his review of *The Prisoner of Zenda* in 1896, 'I might, perhaps, have been satisfied with the sunset scene in the forest of Zenda. . . .' Shaw had more than an art critic's eyes: he had a practical knowledge of stage-lighting techniques. As early as 1894 he was able not only to diagnose what was wrong but to prescribe a remedy as well. Reviewing *Die Walkure* that year, he suggested blowing up the person responsible for lighting the stage, because 'a rock in the foreground, supposed to be illuminated by the sun overhead, throws a strong black shadow *upwards* on a rock behind which is higher than itself . . . this system of black shadows is carried out through the whole scene, destroying all effect of distance, and making the stage look like a mere store-room for dingy canvases'; instead, this person should have 'seen that there were sufficient lights placed on the floor between each set of rocks to overcome the shadow from the footlights and to make the back of the stage look five miles away from the front'. Throughout his theatre reviews, Shaw attacked old-fashioned lighting practices – berating one director, for instance, for modelling his technique on a style of scene painting based on gas illumination instead of making full use of the electric lighting facilities at his disposal.[23]

Shaw kept abreast of developments in stage lighting. In 1905 he called Gordon Craig's design of Ibsen's *The Vikings in Helgeland* 'very instructive as to the possibility of doing away with the eternal . . . footlight illumination which [is] so destructive

22 Simonson, *Part of a Lifetime*, pp. 51-3.
23 *Music in London*, III, 249; *Our Theatres in the Nineties*, I, 172-3; II, 11.

of stage illusion. . . '.[24] That same year he said that the dream scene of *Man and Superman* should be staged 'with top lighting in the manner of Craig'. A dozen years later, he commented that footlighting and top-lighting were equally bad and suggested that the main source of illumination should be the front of the house.[25] In an article supporting the Theatre Guild's fund drive for a new theatre, he urged that 'the stage lighting should be modern, and if possible planned by persons who have never seen footlights, and wonder what on earth they can have been when they read about them in books'.[26]

In his own plays, Shaw used lighting to enhance both theme and theatricality. During the second act of *Mrs Warren's Profession*, after Mrs Warren has won Vivie over with her story of what poverty means, Vivie *'opens the cottage door, and finds that it is broad moonlight'*. Enchanted by the beauty of the night, *'She draws aside the curtains of the window. The landscape is seen bathed in the radiance of the harvest moon rising over Blackdown.'* The act ends with this beautiful, romantic moonlight filling the stage, an ironic comment on the new comradeship between mother and daughter. The next act begins the following morning, *'with the sun shining from a cloudless sky'*, underlining Vivie's new state of mind. When the Devil takes the Statue below in the third act of *Man and Superman*, they stand on the grave-trap. *'It begins to descend slowly. Red glow from the abyss.'* The Statue reminisces: 'Ah, this reminds me of old times.' But Ana cries, 'Stop!' The trap stops part-way down, the red glow illuminating the three – as in the 'old times' – while Ana talks to them briefly. The Epilogue to *Saint Joan* uses projections to enhance the spectacle: *'A vision of the statue in Winchester Cathedral is seen through the window'*, and later, *'A vision of the statue before Rheims Cathedral appears'*. When Joan asks whether she shall rise from the dead and return, there is sudden darkness: only the bed and the figures are visible

---

24 *Pen Portraits and Reviews*, p. 170.

25 Letters: to Florence Farr, Dec. 27, 1905, in Farr *et al.*, *Letters*, p. 34; to William Faversham, April 19, 1917, Hanley Collection.

26 *Shaw on Theatre*, p. 181.

in sillhouette against the light outside the window. At the end of the play, as the clock strikes midnight, '*The last remaining rays of light gather into a white radiance descending on Joan*' while she delivers the final lines: 'O god that madest this beautiful earth, when will it be ready to receive Thy Saints? How long, O Lord, how long?' The illumination descending upon Joan at the end of the play creates a beautiful stage effect and at the same time underscores the play's theme, for Joan is visually alone, set off even from the stage setting.

Shaw's rehearsal notes include the routine, mechanical details of lighting. During rehearsals of *Heartbreak House* he observed that when the curtain rose the lights came up too late and came from the wrong source. A note for *You Never Can Tell* indicated that the front of the stage was too dark; in *Misalliance* there was 'not enough light on the centre clump of flowers'. For the first act of *Arms and the Man*, he wrote that the faces of Raina and Catherine were 'absolutely in the dark', that when Louka opened the door the passage outside was lighter than the stage, that when Raina lighted a candle the electrician should cheat on the light, sneaking up more light than the actual candle would give, and that he should not distractingly change light settings while a scene was in progress: 'Dont fool with the lights: if they are not right, leave them so.'[27]

When others directed his plays, Shaw advised them about the lighting. The arc light in the final act of *Heartbreak House*, he admitted to Lee Simonson, who was to design the play for the Theatre Guild, bothered him from the start. At first, he thought of having a white globe throw a circle of light on the stage floor, 'so that the characters could, as directed, disappear into the surrounding darkness and emerge into the radiance. But, as you say, if you put even a candle in the dark scene the audience can see nothing else.' Since the action called for a visible light that could be visibly extinguished, he thought that Simonson would

27 Rehearsal notes: *Heartbreak House*, 1921, British Museum, Add. 50644; *You Never Can Tell*, undated, British Museum, Add. 50732; *Misalliance*, 1910, Hanley Collection; *Arms and the Man*, 1911, British Museum, Add. 50644.

have to shade the light by draping it ornamentally or putting a green shade around it so as to conceal the actual glare, but do the real lighting from offstage. 'The flagstaff is only an excuse for something characteristic to attach the cable which feeds the arc light. All these things are suggestions and makeshifts.'[28]

COSTUME

In a review of *Romeo and Juliet*, Shaw quoted the programme note, 'Mrs Patrick Campbell's dresses have been carried out by Mrs Mason, of New Burlington Street', and commented, 'I wish they had been carried out and buried. . . . I can only excuse the Lyceum Juliet costumes on the supposition that Mrs Campbell deliberately aimed at suggesting by them the tutelage of a girl of fourteen who is not yet allowed to choose her own dresses'. This quotation is typical of his remarks on costume in his theatre and opera reviews. In the same review, he enunciated one of his major dissatisfactions with costuming in the British theatre: modishness instead of appropriateness. 'I am . . . not surprised to find the dresses at the Lyceum, though handsome and expensive, chastened by the taste of a British gentleman; so that the stalls can contemplate the fourteenth century and yet feel at home there . . .'. He denounced actors and actresses who were 'little more than walking fashion-plates. The actor, in particular, with his carefully ironed new trousers, and his boots conscientiously blackened on the sole underneath the arch of the foot, is a curiously uncomfortable spectacle. . . . I have gradually come to regard the leading man in a play as a set of applied tailor's measurements . . . the clothes having usurped the men's place'. It is pleasant, said Shaw, to look at a lady 'who is characteristically dressed by herself, or affectionately and beautifully dressed by an artist; but fashionable ladies hung with the trophies of their tradesmen are among my strongest aversions . . .'.[29]

Prudery in women's costumes was another aversion. It is

28 Letter to Lee Simonson, Aug. 23, 1920, in Simonson, *Part of a Lifetime*, p. 53.
29 *Our Theatres in the Nineties*, I, 198-9; II, 41-4, 54.

'quite impossible to feel a ray of illusion', Shaw wrote on one occasion, while looking at a Bayreuth Brünhild (*Die Walküre*) climbing the mountains 'with her legs carefully hidden in a long skirt. . . '. To ask the Rhine maidens (*Das Rheingold*) to dress like Rhine maidens might be going too far, he suggested on another occasion, for 'The world is not decent enough for that yet'. But is it necessary for them 'to go to the other extreme and swim about in muslin *fichus* and teagowns?'[30]

Still another pet aversion was a hodge-podge, that is, an absence of artistic costuming. In a production of *Marta*, which takes place at the time of Queen Anne and has her as a character, the ladies were 'in early Victorian Archery Club dresses, the Queen's retinue in the costume of feudal retainers of the Plantagenet period, the comic lord as Sir Peter Teazle, the noblemen in tunics and tights from *Il Trovatore*, and the peasants with huge Bavarian hats beneath their shoulders, reminding one of the men in Othello's yarns'. In a production of *All's Well That Ends Well*, 'The dresses were the usual fancy ball odds and ends, Helena especially distinguishing herself by playing the first scene partly in the costume of Hamlet and partly in that of a waitress in an Aerated Bread Shop. . .'.[31] Such rag-bag costuming was not uncommon.

The major considerations of the costumer, according to Shaw, should be appropriateness to character, social position, situation in the play, and atmosphere. Of a Bayreuth production of Wagner's *Siegfried*, he wrote that the costume of the title character

> is hardly to be described without malice. Imagine an eighteenth-century bank clerk living in a cave, with fashionable sandals and cross garters, an elegant modern classic tunic, a Regent-street bearskin, and a deportment only to be learnt in quadrilles. Or, rather, do not imagine it; but pray that I, who have seen this reality, may not be haunted by it in my

---

30 *Major Critical Essays*, p. 273; *How to Become a Musical Critic*, p. 235.
31 *Music in London*, I, 97; *Our Theatres in the Nineties*, I, 28-9.

dreams. He needed only a tinder-box instead of a furnace, and a patent knife-cleaning machine instead of an anvil, to make him complete.

Realistic costuming is mandatory in Ibsen's dramas, and when reviewing them, Shaw paid special attention to costuming. The 'reckless garments' worn by Nora Helmer, he noted, were 'impossible for a snobbish bank manager's wife. . .'. In *Rosmersholm*, by contrast, Kroll was not dressed well enough: 'I know Kroll by sight perfectly well (was he not for a long time chairman of the London School Board?); and I am certain he would die sooner than pay a visit to the rector in a coat and trousers which would make a superannuated coffee-stall keeper feel apologetic. . .'.[32]

Although Shaw attacked the absence of appropriateness and artistry in stage costuming, he did not neglect to praise them when they were present. In William Poel's production of *Doctor Faustus*, Baliol and Belcher

> were not theatrical devils with huge pasteboard heads, but pictorial Temptation-of-St-Anthony devils such as Martin Schongauer drew. The angels were Florentine fifteenth-century angels, with their draperies sewn into Botticellian folds and tucks. The Emperor's bodyguards had Maximilian-esque uniforms copied from Holbein. Mephistophilis made his first appearance as Mr Joseph Pennell's favorite devil from the roof of Notre Dame. . . .

The Seven Deadly Sins were as *fin de siècle* as possible (*'tout ce qu'il y a de plus fin de siècle'*). 'In short,' Shaw concluded, 'Mr William Poel gave us an artistic rather than a literal presentation of Elizabethan conditions, the result being, as always happens in such cases, that the picture of the past was really a picture of the future. For which result he is, in my judgment, to be highly praised.' On another occasion, Shaw compared Poel's costuming with that of commercial directors who had more money and less

---

32 *How to Become a Musical Critic*, p. 241; *Our Theatres in the Nineties*, I, 73-4; III, 133.

imagination: '. . . our ordinary managers have simply been patronizing the conventional costumier's business in a very expensive way, whilst Mr Poel has achieved artistic originality, beauty, and novelty of effect, as well as the fullest attainable measure of historical conviction.'[33]

Although Shaw was certainly interested in costume, the printed editions of his plays do not have as much costume detail as one might expect. In *The Doctor's Dilemma*, Jennifer's first-act costume is not described at all: Shaw merely noted that Ridgeon *'has an impression that she is very well dressed; but she has a figure on which any dress would look well. . . .'*. In the second act, we are told only that she is *'wrapped up for departure . . .'*. In the third act, she wears a cardinal's robe and hat while modelling for Dubedat, but then takes it off to reveal *'a plain frock of tussore silk'*. In Act IV, she wears *'a nurse's apron'*, and in Act V is *'beautifully dressed . . .'*. Shaw was not always so sparing of detail. See, for example, the costume of The Strange Lady in *The Man of Destiny*:

> *She is not, judging by her dress, an admirer of the latest fashions of the Directory; or perhaps she uses up her old dresses for travelling. At all events she wears no jacket with extravagant lappels, no Greco-Tallien sham chiton, nothing, indeed, that the Princesse de Lamballe might not have worn. Her dress of flowered silk is long waisted, with a Watteau pleat behind, but with the paniers reduced to mere rudiments, as she is too tall for them. It is cut low in the neck, where it is eked out by a creamy fichu.*

With several costumes from which to choose, Shaw selected the most delicate and feminine, thereby ensuring the greater contrast when The Strange Lady dons a soldier's uniform. Without the explicit stage direction, a costumer might select the businesslike *'jacket with extravagant lappels'*, a reasonable choice for a travelling costume, but less feminine than the low-cut, long-waisted, flowered silk dress, and less theatrically effective.

[33] *Our Theatres in the Nineties*, II, 184-5; III, 362.

Shaw was equally adept at describing inelegant dress. In the first act of *Pygmalion*, Liza '*wears a little sailor hat of black straw that has long been exposed to the dust and soot of London and has seldom if ever been brushed. . . . She wears a shoddy black coat that reaches nearly to her knees and is shaped to her waist. She has a brown skirt with a coarse apron. Her boots are much the worse for wear*'. In the second act, '*She has a hat with three ostrich feathers, orange, sky-blue, and red. She has a nearly clean apron, and the shoddy coat has been tidied a little*'. These costume descriptions reveal a great deal about the character and the situation. In the first act, we see the results of Liza's hygienic habits and poverty: her coat is shoddy, her shoes worn out, and her filthy hat may never have been cleaned at all. Her notion of dressing up for a special occasion, we see in the costume description for Act II, consists of wearing cheap, gaudy accessories and cleaning up only somewhat. Her efforts to dress up are both comic and pathetic, for she knows no better. During the play, she learns not only diction but dress and deportment, and her later cleanliness is all the more striking because of the early dirtiness. Her costumes are visual accompaniments to the play's theme.

When it was appropriate, Shaw also described characteristic men's costumes. Marchbanks enters in the first act of *Candida* wearing apparel that Shaw called '*anarchic. He wears an old blue serge jacket, unbuttoned, over a woollen lawn tennis shirt, with a silk handerchief for a cravat, trousers matching the jacket, and brown canvas shoes. In these garments he has apparently lain in the heather and waded through the waters; and there is no evidence of his having ever brushed them.*' Apollodorus, in *Caesar and Cleopatra*, is aestheticism personified, apparently as *fin de siècle* as William Poel's Seven Deadly Sins. He is '*dressed with deliberate aestheticism in the most delicate purples and dove greys, with ornaments of bronze, oxydized silver, and stones of jade and agate. His sword, designed as carefully as a medieval cross, has a blued blade shewing through an openwork scabbard of purple leather and filagree.*' Marchbanks' clothes indicate the Bohemian poet, Apollodorus' the devotee of 'Art for Art's sake'.

While Shaw's textual commentaries on costumes were generally sparse, he made up for it in his personal dealings with actors, directors, and costumers. In *Fanny's First Play*, Count O'Dowda and his daughter are described as wearing costumes '*a hundred years out of date*'. Shaw explained his general ideas to Charles Ricketts, who was designing costumes for this play.

> Now one of the Count's repudiations of modern civilization takes the form of refusing to wear modern dress because it is ugly. When he appears in the Induction simply in front of a black tableau curtain, he may wear any dress of any country and any period or of no country and no period, provided it dates before 1830. I vaguely conceived him as a Venetian eighteenth-century *père noble*, somewhere between Guardi and Goya, but I was utterly unable to reduce this conception to anything definite. . . .
>
> Then there is the daughter. She is to be played by Christine Silver, who has a very slim pretty girlish figure of the Canova sort. I had an idea of making her one of those *fillettes* that one sees on French eighteenth-century crockery of the most elegant pre-revolutionary period; but though I rushed through the Wallace Collection and then through the Victoria and Albert Museum, from one end to the other, I could not find a single specimen of what I wanted.[34]

When faced with a production, Shaw was forced to be precise – even to the point of drawing costume sketches for *Arms and the Man* (see Figures 8–11). 'Dont muddle about mid-Victorian costumes,' he advised Molly Tompkins, who was to appear in *You Never Can Tell*; 'take the exact date (1895?) and look up the volumes of *Punch* for that year: the DuMaurier pictures will give you the fashions.'[35] In *Captain Brasshound's Conversion* Lady Cicely dresses as she would in Surrey and does not wear a

[34] Letter to Charles Ricketts, April 10, 1911, in Charles Ricketts, *Self-Portrait*, ed. Cecil Lewis (London: Peter Davies, 1939), pp. 162-3.

[35] Postal card, Feb. 15, 1922, in *Shaw-Tompkins*, p. 19. *You Never Can Tell* takes place in 1896.

Figures 1–5. *The Devil's Disciple.*

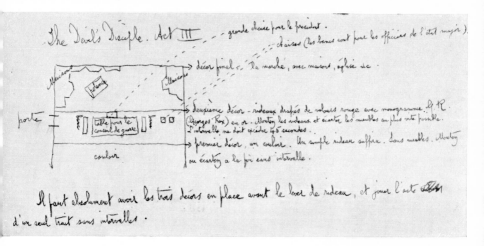

Figure 5. Plan of Act III, Scenes 1, 2, 3, the three scenes separated by curtains.

Beneath the plan, Shaw writes, 'It is absolutely necessary that the three sets be in place before the curtain rises, and that the act be played in one stretch, without any breaks'.

Downstage is the first scene, a 'lobby'. To the side of the plan, Shaw writes, 'first set, a lobby. A simple curtain will suffice. Without furniture. Raise or separate [the curtains] at the end without a break'.

Above this is the second scene. On stage right is a 'door'. At stage centre is a 'table for the court martial'. On either side is a 'bench'. Above the table is a 'large chair for the president [of the council]'. On stage left are two 'chairs (the benches are for the officers of the general staff)'. To the side of the plan, Shaw writes, 'second act – curtains hung with red velour with monogram G.R. (George Rex) in gold. Raise the curtain and strike the furniture as quickly as possible. The time break should not exceed 45 seconds'.

Upstage is the third scene. At upstage right and left are 'Houses'. Up right centre is 'gallows'. To the side, Shaw writes, 'final set. the procession, with houses, church &c.'.

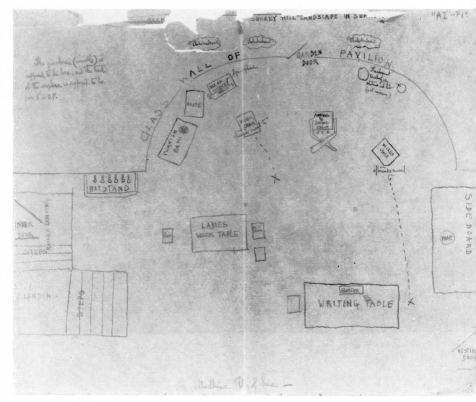

Figure 6. Ground plan (by Shaw) of *Misalliance*, for William Faversham's 1917 production in the United States (in Hanley Collection, Academic Center Library, University of Texas).

The writing is in Shaw's hand. Upper left hand corner: 'The gramophone (invisible) is supposed to be here, and the track of the aeroplane is supposed to be from P. to O.P. [stage right to stage left]'. Upstage: 'Back Cloth', 'Surrey Hill Landscape in Summer'. Below: three clumps of 'Rhododendrons'. Below the glass wall, the small script seems to read 'Gramophone', 'Flamboyant Crockery or statues ad lib. (not necessary)'. Both wicker chairs are 'afterwards moved to X'.

tailor-made tourist's costume because 'she is too conventional to regard dress as a wholly adaptable-to-circumstances matter. She would wear petticoats and drawers, just as she would say her prayers, for half a century after all the working women in the country would have taken to knickerbockers and agnosticism.'[36] Shaw provided Granville Barker with a list of costumes and costume accessories for *The Admirable Bashville*, including 'A gorgeous livery with tags, plush smalls, calves, and a heavily powdered wig for Bashville. The wig is important, as when he says O Bathos! in his great soliloquy he must strike his head and send up a cloud of powder from it.' He suggested that Barker borrow one of painter Neville Lytton's thoroughly dirtied old painting smocks to wear as Dubedat in *The Doctor's Dilemma*. The Beadle's costume in *Getting Married* 'must not be a comic one out of sketches by Boz. A modern Borough Council Beadle is rather like a fashionable music hall chucker-out. The cocked hat still exists; and there is a short caped Inverness with gold braid; but the rest is an immaculate frock coat and trousers with gold braid & stripe down the leg. . . . The mace may be *ad lib*.' In the first scene of *Saint Joan*, Baudricourt and Poulengey 'should be in half armor and be obviously soldiers and not merchants. This is important, as it strikes the note of France in war. . . . Poulengey's coat should not be belted [as it was in the Theatre Guild production]. Baudricourt should be smart, a *beau sabreur*.'[37]

Shaw's rehearsal notes regarding costumes sometimes merely expressed dissatisfaction: Mrs Clandon's costume, for instance, he called 'appallingly wrong – dress contradicts her part'. On other occasions, they either implied or explicitly stated the remedy. Gunner should have a 'celluloid collar'. For *Man and Superman*, Ann must 'have a hat – she looks too old. ?Flowers in hair or at waist'. In *Arms and the Man*, Bluntschli's uniform

---

[36] *Shaw on Theatre*, p. 82.

[37] Letters: Shaw to Granville Barker, May 26, 1903, in *Shaw-Barker*, p. 14; Barker to Neville Lytton, Oct. 12, 1906, Berg Collection; Shaw to J. E. Vedrenne, April 26, 1908, Hanley Collection; Shaw to Lawrence Langner, Feb. 1, 1924, in Langner, *G.B.S.*, p. 74.

L

was 'not torn enough', and in *Pygmalion*, Liza's dressing-gown should have been blue and white, and smaller.[38]

Clearly, Shaw did not neglect costuming, but rather paid a great deal of attention to it. He researched historical costumes, and on some occasions gave detailed descriptions. In a few instances, he carefully described modern costumes. Although his printed specifications on dress are, for the most part, far less precise than his descriptions of scenery, they are adequate guides to the costumer who must provide a specific actress (or actor) with attractive or unattractive, but (in either case) characteristic clothing, the selection of which can vary greatly from one actress to the next, for what will enhance a particular actress's beauty may very well destroy another actress's good looks. As a director, however, with actual people to costume, Shaw was exact.

MAKE-UP

As a director, Shaw scrutinized make-up (including wigs), for he knew its value in convincing the audience of the reality of the character. Most of his statements on this subject are characteristically pragmatic and concern the make-up of a particular actor or actress. As an opera and theatre critic, Shaw pointed out those instances where the make-up spoiled the dramatic illusion. He recalled having seen Celeste

> as the heroine of a melodrama in which she was eighteen in the first act, thirty in the second, forty in the third, sixty in the fourth, and eighty in the fifth; after which I came away wondering how old Madame really was, as she had looked like a made-up old woman in the early stages, and like a made-up young woman in the later ones, never by any chance presenting a convincing appearance of being near the age indicated by the dramatist.

[38] Rehearsal notes: *You Never Can Tell*, undated, Texas; *Misalliance*, 1910, Hanley Collection; *Man and Superman*, 1907, British Museum, Add. 50735; *Arms and the Man*, 1911, Texas; *Pygmalion*, 1914, Hanley Collection.

When Wilson Barrett appeared in *The Sign of the Cross*, he neglected to wear an appropriate wig. Instead of the cropped Roman hairdo, 'he wears his own hair in his old familiar feminine fashion, with the result that when he first steps on the stage he presents such an amazing resemblance to Miss Victor that, instead of applauding him, I stared with a shocked conviction that I had that lady before me in the costume of a Roman warrior'.[39]

During productions of his own plays, he attended closely to the make-up. He told Janet Achurch, who had recently become a blonde, that in order to play Candida she must immediately

send for a barber, and have your head shaved absolutely bald. Then get a brown wig, of the natural color of your own hair. Candida with gold hair is improbable; but Candida with artificially gold hair is impossible. Further, you must not be fringy or fluffy. Send to a photograph shop for a picture of some Roman bust – say that of Julia, daughter of Augustus and wife of Agrippa, from the Uffizi in Florence – and take that as your model, or rather as your point of departure. You must part your hair in the middle, and be sweet, sensible, comely, dignified, and Madonna like. If you condescend to the vulgarity of being a pretty woman, much less a flashy one . . . you are lost.

For Elder Daniels in *The Shewing-up of Blanco Posnet*, he suggested 'an Abraham Lincoln get-up'. For the Dauphin in *Saint Joan*, the wig should be modelled on a portrait of the real Dauphin, which demonstrates that 'his hair was completely concealed by the fashion of the time, giving him a curiously starved and bald appearance that would be very effective on the stage'.[40]

As a director of his own plays, Shaw realized that the make-up could assist or spoil the dramatic illusion. His rehearsal notes contain practical suggestions on make-up. When Higgins calls

[39] *Music in London*, III, 70; *Our Theatres in the Nineties*, II, 14.
[40] Letters: to Janet Achurch, March 20, 1895, in *Collected Letters*, p. 502; to Martin Harvey, Nov. 26, 1926, Houghton Library, Harvard College; to Lawrence Langner, Feb. 1, 1924, in Langner, *G.B.S.*, p. 75.

Liza 'so horribly dirty', Shaw asked Mrs Patrick Campbell, 'How can [he] say that to such a make-up?'[41] He noted that Broadbent's make-up was too young, and that Mrs Higgins' was too old. Lord Summerhays, he suggested, needed a 'touch of pink in the make-up'. He advised the Raina of 1911 that her left eyebrow was ragged, and the Raina of 1919 that the rouge on her cheeks should continue up to her eyes.[42] Hairpieces, too, came under Shaw's scrutiny: he noted that in *Man and Superman*, 'Malone's wig [was] too short', that in *Heartbreak House*, Shotover might have 'whiskers like Ibsen', and that in *Caesar and Cleopatra*, Britannus 'must have Dundreary whiskers – yellow whiskers'. His 'wig, moustache and whiskers can all be made on a frame which he can put on like a helmet: it cannot be stuck on with spirit gum'.[43] In short, Shaw not only gave his attention to the actors' make-up, but had enough practical knowledge of make-up to be able to specify a remedy when he noted a shortcoming.

MUSIC

As one would expect of a director who had been a music critic, Shaw was precise about the use of music in plays. He deplored Augustin Daly's use of music in *Twelfth Night* as 'a curious example of the theatrical tradition that any song written by Shakespear is appropriate to any play written by him, except, perhaps, the play in which it occurs'. Insisting on the appropriateness of the music to the play, to the situation, and, if sung, to both the character who sings it and to his audience, Shaw derided as an 'absurdity' the opening scene of the production: '. . . the entry of all the lodging-house keepers (as I presume)on

41 Rehearsal notes, *Pygmalion*, 1914, Hanley Collection.

42 Rehearsal notes: *John Bull's Other Island*, 1907, British Museum, Add. 50736; *Pygmalion*, 1920, British Museum, Add. 50644; *Misalliance*, 1910, Hanley Collection; *Arms and the Man*, 1911, British Museum, Add. 50644; *Arms and the Man*, 1919, Burgunder Collection.

43 Rehearsal notes: *Man and Superman*, 1907, British Museum, Add. 50735; *Heartbreak House*, 1929, British Museum, Add. 50647; letters to Gabriel Pascal, July 26 and 28, 1944, in Deans, *Meeting at the Sphinx*, pp. 37-8.

Figure 7. Perspective sketch (by Shaw) of *Misalliance*, for William Faversham's 1917 production in the United States (in the Hanley Collection, Academic Center Library, University of Texas). The writing is in Shaw's hand.

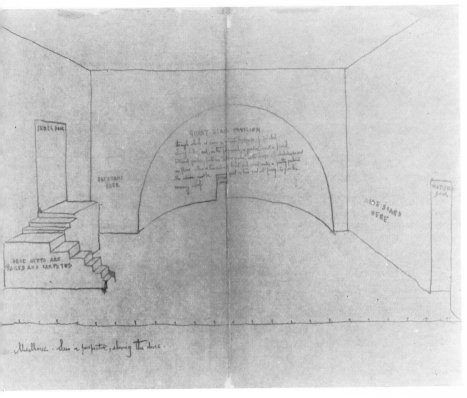

Misalliance. Scene in perspective, showing the doors'.

Upstage centre: 'great glass pavilion through which is seen a distant landscape of fir clad Surrey hills, and, in the foreground, a garden – not a formal terraced garden, but an "A [illegible] garden", with clumps of rhododendrons in flower. This is the centre of light and must make a pretty picture. The interior must be quiet in tone and not fussy, to give the necessary relief'. In the centre aperture: 'garden door'.

Figures 8–11. Costume sketches (by Shaw) for 1894 production of *Arms and the Man* (in the British Museum, Add. 50603).* The writing, except as noted for Figure 11, is in Shaw's hand.

Figure 8. Upper left hand corner: 'Bluntschli'. Bottom: 'Servian Artillery Captain'.

*Another set of these drawings is in the Burgunder Collection, Cornell University. Alison Kerr, reporting the identification of the drawings as Shaw's for the 1894 production, adds that they 'were reproduced by the "jellygraph" process, an early means of duplication'. See *Bernard Shaw: An Exhibition of Books and Manuscripts from the Collection Presented by Mr Bernard Burgunder Cornell 1918* (Ithaca, N.Y.: Cornell University Library, 1963), p. 9.

the sea-coast of Illyria to sing Ariel's song from The Tempest, Come unto these yellow sands'. 'On the other hand,' said Shaw, 'the introduction of the serenade from Cymbeline at the end of the third act, with Who is Sylvia? altered to Who's Olivia? seems to me to be quite permissible, as it is neither an interpolation nor an alteration, but a pure interlude, and a very attractive one . . .'. In Daly's production of *Two Gentlemen of Verona*,

> the most horribly common music repeatedly breaks out on the slightest pretext or on no pretext at all. One dance, set to a crude old English popular tune, sundry eighteenth and nineteenth century musical banalities, and a titivated plantation melody in the first act which produces an indescribably atrocious effect by coming in behind the scenes as a sort of coda to Julia's curtain speech, all turn the play . . . into a vaudeville. Needless to add, the accompaniments are not played on lutes and viols, but by the orchestra and a guitar or two. In the forest scene the outlaws begin the act by a chorus. After their encounter with Valentine they go off the stage singing the refrain exactly in the style of La Fille de Madame Angot.

Shaw called this 'wanton absurdity'.[44]

When he asked for music in his plays, he was exact, specifying such works as *Don Giovanni* and Gounod's *Faust* for the Hell scene of *Man and Superman*, 'Keep the Home Fires Burning' as the bombs fall in *Heartbreak House*, 'Oh, Won't You Come Home, Bill Bailey?' (sung by a chorus of angels) in *Passion, Poison, and Petrifaction*, and the Wedding Chorus from Donizetti's *Lucia di Lammermoor* as Barbara's heart is breaking in the second act of *Major Barbara*.

On a few occasions, he gave instructions regarding instrumentation. In the prefatory note to *Passion, Poison, and Petrifaction*, Shaw specified an orchestra of 'at least a harp, a drum, and a pair of cymbals'. And he was precise in instructions to directors of *Caesar and Cleopatra*:

[44] *Music in London*, III, 140-1; *Our Theatres in the Nineties*, I, 174.

The sound of the bucina and the trumpet calls must not, even at hopelessly third rate provincial representations, be represented by hackneyed flourishes on the cornet. A trombone for the bucina and a couple of cavalry trumpets can always be procured with a little trouble. Where proper arrangements can be made, as in London, by the conductor of the orchestra, he should be empowered to specially engage a few players who can handle the long trumpet. . . . Perhaps the best instrument to represent the bucina is the ophicleide, which gives a peculiar bullock-like bellow, but as it is hard to find ophicleide players now-a-days, the bombardon (E flat tuba – or B flat, if one can be got) is likely to be the practicable alternative. A powerful low note from such an instrument, answered by a flourish on an alto trombone, and leading to several ringing high notes from the long trumpets, would be the sort of thing for the alarums. On no account should a cornet be heard on the stage.[45]

When Shaw prepared the first production of *The Dark Lady of the Sonnets*, he called for music at several points:

1. A prelude to take up the curtain and exhibit the sky and the warder. My notion is simply a long-sustained mysterious note on the bassoon and the Westminster chimes presently played in single notes by the harp, which will finally strike the hour on its lowest E (I think Big Ben is in E). The music stops when the warder challenges Shakespear.

2. A shimmering from the fiddles when the light heralds Elizabeth, continuing more or less until she wakes, when it stops abruptly.

3. I am not quite sure about this; but there might be some music when the Dark Lady enters, rising rapidly to a climax and breaking off when she boxes their ears.

4. The Westminster chimes again as at first at the end, as Shakespear is led off by the warder. . . . I shall get the warder

---

[45] 'Notes to Act I [of *Caesar and Cleopatra*]', Berg Collection.

to lead Shakespear off whilst Elizabeth retires to her original ray of light. In short, a very quiet 'Exeunt severally', stealing off to mysterious music.[46]

When Shaw used an orchestra, he took care that it did not alter his plans. After attending a performance of *Annajanska*, he asked Lillah McCarthy, who played the title role, 'What is the matter with the band? . . . why on earth dont they give the last 13 bars of the overture at the end full crash instead of piffling as they do?'[47]

In summation, to say that Shaw did not pay much attention to the technical side of play production is inaccurate. Vitally concerned with this aspect of theatre, he knew that obvious make-up, inadequate lighting, makeshift scenery, inappropriate music, and the like, could destroy any illusion of reality that the author and actor might otherwise create. Detesting clichés, shoddy execution, and lack of credibility in stage scenery, lighting, and costuming, Shaw aimed for beauty, harmony, illusion, and appropriateness to the play's themes, moods, and characters. Moreover, he kept up with new developments in scene design and lighting, drawing upon those which he found useful. 'Art is one and indivisible,' he said to Ellen Terry when he tried to impress upon her the importance of stage scenery. The statement might be taken as a Shavian maxim. For Shaw the director, art was indeed a unified, indivisible entity. He worried about the lighting plot and the eyebrow pencil as he worried about a line-reading, for he understood that all are components of the total art of the theatre, and all are the province of the director, who employs them in his efforts to realize the play on stage.

[46] Letter to Charles Ricketts, Nov. 21, 1910, in Ricketts, *Self-Portrait*, pp. 154-5.
[47] Letter to Lillah McCarthy, Jan. 25, 1918, in McCarthy, *Myself and My Friends*, p. 192.

VII

The Business of Theatre

Shaw was a complete 'man of the theatre', a director and play-wright who involved himself in every aspect of theatrical activity – including finances, promotion and publicity, and even front-of-house operations. Our study should therefore consider him in relation to these aspects.

In his preface to William Archer's *The Theatrical 'World' of 1894*, Shaw wrote that 'the art of the theatre is as dependent on its business as a poet's genius is on his bread and butter'.[1] Shaw himself was an astute businessman. According to Lawrence Langner, every time Shaw and the Theatre Guild had a difference of opinion about a business matter, 'he almost invariably turned out to be right'.[2]

Shaw's wealth (by the time of his death he had amassed over a million dollars) was partially a result of his absolute refusal to sell or assign his copyrights. To producers and publishers, he granted only licences for fixed periods of time. If he suspected his rights were being violated by surreptitious performances of his work, or by pirated editions, he ascertained whether this was the case, and, if so, retaliated with every legal means at his disposal.

His first job – for the Dublin firm of Uniacke Townshend and Company – included handling large sums of money and keeping accounts of receipts and expenditures. The business skills acquired there served him throughout his life. He kept careful records of all his financial transactions and the laws relating to these transactions – no small undertaking, since national boundaries were crossed. He maintained records of weekly and some-times daily gross receipts, as well as his author's share, on all

1 *Shaw on Theatre*, p. 42.
2 Langner, *G.B.S.*, p. 191.

of his plays that were being performed on several continents. These figures were in pounds, shillings, and even pence. After Charlotte Payne-Townshend married Shaw, she took charge of his ledgers, and later a secretary performed this task, but Shaw carefully examined the ledgers.[3] 'An author should always have these [box-office] returns', he explained to Siegfried Trebitsch, 'not only to check the accounts, but to be able to follow the history of his play – whether it is getting more or less popular, whether it is gaining with the gallery and losing with the stalls (so as to shew the class of people it appeals to), and also to be able to shew them to managers in making fresh contracts as proof of the previous successes of the author'.[4]

To protect themselves against the unscrupulous business practices of German publishers, Shaw suggested that he and Trebitsch might do their own printing of the German editions of Shaw's works and have Cotta or another publisher sell them on a commission basis; in this case, Trebitsch must stipulate that *he* would order and pay for the printing: 'Otherwise the publisher will produce receipts from the printer and bookbinder for sums on which he has been allowed a discount of 20 or 30 per cent, and we shall be cheated. It is worth while fighting out these details, as it will save you a great deal of time and trouble afterwards. When Cotta learns that you know the tricks of trade, he will not waste your time trying them on you.' Aware of the tricks of trade, even of international trade, Shaw urged Trebitsch, after the First World War, to keep the money for Shaw's royalties in a Vienna account until the rate of exchange improved. He was also aware of the tricks of copyright. A chapter in *The Irrational Knot* had been 'purposely so altered in the new edition that an attempt to pirate the new edition under cover of the old [which was out of copyright] can be immediately detected and proved...'.[5]

3 Financial records are in the Hanley Collection and the British Museum, Add. 50649 and 50731. Some of the accounts that Charlotte Shaw kept for her husband have been published in Janet Dunbar, *Mrs G.B.S.* (London: Harrap, 1963), pp. 188, 223.

4 Letter to Siegfried Trebitsch, June 16, 1904, Berg Collection.

5 *Ibid.*, Dec. 13, 1904, Nov. 21, 1907, April 19, 1921.

He drove a hard bargain, and demanded royalties on a sliding scale geared to the gross receipts of each performance. The particular figures in the scale varied, changing in Shaw's favour as his plays became more popular.[6] In the United States, he often did business at a straight 10 per cent, but, he said, 'this may be regarded as a minimum', and 'a good deal depends on the manager with whom I am dealing'.[7] In order to prevent managers from taking a play in order to keep someone else from producing it, Shaw stipulated that if the play were not produced by a specified date, or if it were immediately withdrawn before the total payments amounted to a certain sum, that amount was forfeited to him. In 1916, the amount was five hundred pounds (or twenty-five hundred dollars).[8]

Shaw had a reputation for being inexorable about his sliding scale. Lawrence Langner complained that since it cost at least fifteen thousand dollars per week to run one of Shaw's plays,

[6] The following samples indicate the evolution of Shaw's prosperity and power. In 1894, when *Arms and the Man* played at the Avenue Theatre, he was to receive 10 per cent of the gross nightly receipts when they exceeded £150, 7½ per cent when they exceeded £100 but did not exceed £150, and 5 per cent when they did not exceed £100. (Letter to Henry Arthur Jones, April 24, 1894, in Jones, *Taking the Curtain Call*, p. 128.) This did *not* mean 5 percent of the first £100, 7½ per cent of the next £50, and so forth. If the gross receipts were £100, his percentage was 5 per cent, but if they were £100 and one shilling, he received 7½ per cent of the *entire* gross, if £150 and one shilling, 10 per cent of the entire gross. By 1900 his fees went up. He was to receive 12 per cent of the gross nightly receipts when they exceeded £150, 10 per cent when they exceeded £100 but did not exceed £150, 7½ per cent when they exceeded £50 but did not exceed £100, and 5 per cent when they did not exceed £50. (Draft of an Agreement between Shaw and Johnston Forbes-Robertson, 1900, Hanley Collection.) By 1916, his fees had gone up to 15 per cent when the gross nightly receipts exceeded £300 (in the United States, when they exceeded $1,500), 10 per cent when they exceeded £100 (or $500) but did not exceed £300 (or $1,500), 7½ per cent when they exceeded £50 (or $250) but did not exceed £100 (or $500), and 5 per cent when they did not exceed £50 (or $250). (Draft of an Agreement between Shaw and the Theatre Guild, 1916, in Langner, *G.B.S.*, p. 298; Memorandum of an Agreement between Shaw and Mrs Virginia Compton, 1918, Yale University Library.)

For one-act plays, Shaw's rule was a discount of half if there were another copyright play on the same bill, a discount of two-thirds if there were two other copyright plays on the bill. If there were no other copyright plays on the bill, he demanded full fees. (Letter to Mrs H. H. Champion, May 18, 1926, Hanley Collection.)

[7] Letter to R. E. Golding Bright, Oct. 22, 1913, in *Advice to a Young Critic*, p. 193; Draft of an Agreement between Shaw and Richard Mansfield, 1894, Berg Collection; Memorandum of an Agreement between Shaw and Robert Loraine, 1905, Hanley Collection.

[8] Langner, *G.B.S.*, p. 298.

the author's 15 per cent royalty was too high. Shaw promptly offered his plays royalty free up to fifteen thousand dollars, with a fifty-fifty split over that sum. Langner, of course, refused, for the author's share would come to much more on that basis.[9] Although Shaw fostered the impression that he was absolutely intractable on the subject of author's royalties, this was not actually so. When Mrs Patrick Campbell toured *Pygmalion* in the United States, he worked out a kickback arrangement whereby he would remit half of his fees to her when receipts fell to eight hundred pounds a week.[10] His motive might have been friendship, or a desire to keep his play running even if it meant playing to only moderate-sized houses, or possibly both. It was certainly worth more to him in the long run to keep the Court Theatre in operation than to squeeze as much as possible from a single play, for he was that company's chief playwright and the company had actors sympathetic to and proficient in performing his plays. He therefore gave them every possible concession.[11] When the Court seasons ended in June 1907, Shaw arranged for a season at the Savoy Theatre, guaranteeing two thousand pounds, to be repaid on net profits which were to be reckoned after charging Vedrenne's and Barker's salaries (£1000 a year each) as expenses. His own salary, he said, would 'be taken out in moral superiority'.[12] On other occasions, Shaw reasonably agreed to a 5 per cent royalty in places where the higher percentages would prevent the play from being done.[13] And he sometimes made arrangements for weekly or fixed fees.[14]

For amateurs, there were different terms. The 'old style' amateurs – that is, the nonprofessionals who would get up a

9 *Ibid.*, p. 182.

10 Letter to Mrs Patrick Campbell, May 15, 1915, in *Shaw-Campbell*, p. 196.

11 He made special arrangements with Vedrenne, for example, that the six matinees of *John Bull's Other Island* and the six of *Candida* would give him a royalty of 10 per cent only if the gross receipts exceeded £600 (as opposed to £100 or £150 elsewhere), 7½ per cent if they were over £300 and 5 per cent if £300 and below (as opposed to over and under £50 elsewhere). See letter to J. E. Vedrenne, Oct. 26, 1904, Hanley Collection.

12 Letter to Granville Barker, July 27, 1907, in *Shaw-Barker*, pp. 91-2.

13 Letter to R. E. Golding Bright, Nov. 16, 1904, in *Advice to a Young Critic*, p. 156.

14 Memorandum of Agreement between Shaw and Roy Limbert, 1938, Berg Collection; letter to Sir John Martin-Harvey, Oct. 26, 1928, Houghton Library, Harvard College.

performance for a charity benefit – had to pay five guineas (five pounds, five shillings) per performance, or eight guineas for two performances. But if amateurs decided to compete with professionals – for example, taking a major Dublin theatre to present premieres of Shaw plays – Shaw refused them amateur terms: to take Dublin's Gaiety Theatre, 'present a play which has not been judged in that city by a professional performance, and claim amateur terms, is absurd'.[15] When a new type of amateur appeared, devoted to the art of the theatre and trying to produce plays where professionals would not go, Shaw recognized this change and altered his fees accordingly. He sympathized with the new amateurs, who presented the new drama at a price the people could afford, perhaps taking in a total of fifteen shillings at the gate. Under such circumstances, he thought it unreasonable to demand five guineas. Instead, he charged them a percentage of the gate, and if that percentage came to ninepence, he would tip his hat, thank them, and sincerely ask for a renewal of their favours.[16] Still, he did not wish to have advantage taken of him. If these new amateurs organized theatre clubs, admitted members free, and charged nonmembers, Shaw demanded that his percentage include the seats occupied by the members.[17]

As a trade-unionist, however, Shaw would not undersell foreign competitors, for he wanted all playwrights to have a decent minimum wage. Even though it was difficult enough for a playwright to live on 10 per cent, he explained to Trebitsch, a manager in a foreign country would, if he could, offer the native playwright 4 per cent, telling him that if he did not take it the manager would get an English play for 4 per cent. Shaw therefore ascertained the highest percentage paid to native authors, and then demanded more. 'In Denmark they told me that no Danish author ever got more than 6 per cent; and they offered me 5. I said $7\frac{1}{2}$. They said it was utterly impossible. I

15 Letters to R. E. Golding Bright, April 6, 1904 and March 3, 1907, in *Advice to a Young Critic*, pp. 143, 179.

16 *Shaw on Theatre*, pp. 230-5.

17 Letters: to H. H. Champion, Dec. 14, 1911, Hanley Collection; to Maurice Browne, March 17, 1915, Hanley Collection.

stuck to it like a mule. They gave in; and now the Danish authors bless me for putting up prices.'[18]

While Shaw drove a hard bargain, he was not rapacious to the extent of being unfair to his friends and supporters. Refusing to give rights for the United States premiere of *John Bull's Other Island* to anyone but Arnold Daly, Shaw told his agent: 'Daly has done very well with my plays: why should I now wantonly throw him over & let the other fellows profit by his risk & his devotion? Tell your man to go away & write a play for himself if he wants one.' When Robert Loraine had a success in *Cyrano de Bergerac* in 1919, he sent a cheque to Shaw for an outstanding debt on royalties from the Canadian tour of *Man and Superman*, seven years earlier. Shaw replied:

> The £600 or whatever it is is all nonsense. The play did not make the money. Now, if your acting had lost it, and I could contend that the money was there for you to make had you been equal to the occasion, I should claim it remorselessly. But the facts as compared with runs elsewhere prove that your acting made more money than the play, and of this surplus I had a very substantial whack.
>
> There is consequently no real human reason why I should exploit you and Rostand (or another) for money that the wretched *Superman* never earned. The Statute of Limitations which has already written off the item legally is for once right as well as convenient.

And when *Fanny's First Play* became, as Shaw put it, 'the *Charley's Aunt* of the new drama', he told Charles Ricketts, who designed costumes for the play, of the fortune he had received in author's fees:

> As this clearly changes a desperate artistic enterprise into a sordid commercial speculation, I can see no mortal reason why you should design dresses for it for nothing. I therefore, with the brutal indelicacy of a successful man, ask you what

18 Letter to Siegfried Trebitsch, Aug. 18, 1906, Berg Collection.

is your tariff for designing dresses. . . . Tell me what I ought to pay you, and I will give you 5 per cent of it, as, if you put it anywhere near the truth, I shall not be able to afford any more.

Ricketts, not to be outdone, asked Shaw to accept the costumes as a 'cheap *beau geste* . . . the natural neighbourly act of one art to another'.[19]

But Shaw did not use his business knowledge only to drive bargains for royalties. Since he wanted his plays to get large audiences and to make money for all concerned, he examined the numerous factors affecting these objectives. *You Never Can Tell* had played six matinees at the Strand Theatre early in May 1900. When Frank Curzon, manager of the Strand, proposed that Yorke Stephens (who had played Valentine) revive the play at the end of May, Shaw refused. 'Our profits', he told Stephens, 'are easily computed: there wont be any'. He then instructed Stephens to

> Tell Mr Curzon that no play of mine is going into an evening bill at the end of May, under any circumstances whatever, short of an advance of £2,500 to the author. The 25th March is my latest date for a summer production, and the first of September my earliest for a winter one.
>
> If he cares to make a serious proposal for a regular production in September, with certain comparatively expensive changes in the cast, new scenery, and everything firstrate, I am open to that or anything else in the regular way of business, though I shouldnt advise him to do anything of the sort, because nothing but a very stylish production at a very stylish theatre, with handsome advertising, will give the play a chance. But in any case no fresh move can be made at the West End before September.[20]

19 Letters: Shaw to R. E. Golding Bright, March 8, 1905, in *Advice to a Young Critic*, pp. 161-2; Shaw to Robert Loraine, no date given, in Loraine, *Head Wind*, p. 267; Shaw to Charles Ricketts, Oct. 7, 1911, and Charles Ricketts to Shaw, October, 1911 (no day given), in Ricketts, *Self-Portrait*, pp. 167-8.
20 Letter to Yorke Stephens, May 21, 1900, Enthoven Collection.

He urged Ada Rehan, who was contemplating a production of *Captain Brassbound's Conversion* in the United States, to play it in London first, for a success in one country may not mean a success in the other.

Now the failure of a London success in America does nobody any harm except the manager, because it is always claimed that a play good enough for London is good enough for anywhere, and that the Americans ought to be ashamed of themselves for not appreciating it.

BUT – and this is important – the failure of an American success in London is bad for everybody, because it is attributed at once to the superior taste of London.

Moral: always try London first. If you succeed, no subsequent failure can discredit your success or lower your prestige in the part. If you dont succeed, the management has a far stronger interest in keeping the piece on and nursing it as an apparent success for America & the provinces than in the case of an American production. If you fail, you can still try America far more easily and hopefully than you could try London after an American failure. And you can win in London what is called a moral victory: that is, if your venture is recognized at aiming high, you can come out of a financial failure with an enhanced reputation, whereas in America nothing succeeds but financial success.[21]

He informed Trebitsch that unless a star actress who was both extraordinarily popular and extraordinarily good, were engaged for *Pygmalion*, failure would be certain, and he warned William Faversham that too many high-priced actors for *Getting Married* would mean financial ruin, since their drawing powers would overlap, and there were only so many people in New York willing to see this type of play.[22] The opening of *John Bull's Other Island*, he advised Barker, must not take place until after Parliament met in the fall, for the political people would fill the

21 Letter to Ada Rehan, Aug. 30, 1904, Hanley Collection.
22 Letters: to Siegfried Trebitsch, Jan. 29, 1913, Berg Collection; to William Faversham, April 7, 1916, Hanley Collection.

theatre. The opening of *Heartbreak House,* he told the Theatre Guild, must be delayed until after the November elections in the United States:

> It would be far better to produce *H.H.* with the first cast you could pick out of the gutter on the 15th of Nov. than to produce it on the 15th of October with Sarah Bernhardt, the two Guitrys, Edwin Drew, Maude Adams, Charlie Chaplin and Mary Pickford.
>
> A running play may do very well, because people already know about it, and it needs no press. But a new production has no chance. The presidential candidates play the author and the cast off the stage: and the election crowds out the theatre. If you doubt me, try – but with somebody else's play. You will never try again.

Langner admitted that it took the Theatre Guild several years to learn how right Shaw was.[23]

Well aware of the fact that promotion and publicity affect the box-office, Shaw often took charge of these matters. Sometimes, he composed journalistically factual press releases: 'Please note that the forthcoming revival of Mr Bernard Shaw's Arms & The Man under Mr F. C. Whitney's management will take place at the Criterion Theatre on Thursday the 18th May', with the cast, the time of performance, and the theatre's phone number.[24] At other times, his publicity releases were in the usual Shavian style: 'This morning,' he wrote to Trebitsch, 'I sent an article to Die Zeit of the most Shawish description, full of the most insufferable egotism, and warning the Viennese against Candida. Also explaining that the Teufelskerl [*The Devil's Disciple*] is all state melodrama.'[25] He was concerned that the audience know exactly when a play was being performed if it did not run on

23 Letters: to Granville Barker, Aug. 20, 1904, in *Shaw-Barker,* p. 25; to Lawrence Langner, no date given, in Langner, *G.B.S.,* pp. 25-6.

24 Pencil draft of publicity release for revival of *Arms and the Man* at the Criterion Theatre, May 18, 1911, British Museum, Add. 50644.

25 Postcard to Siegfried Trebitsch, Feb. 14, 1903, Berg Collection. See also *Advice to a Young Critic, passim.*

consecutive days. For Barker's matinees of *Candida*, Shaw insisted that 'Unless every advertisement is headed TUESDAYS THURSDAYS and FRIDAYS in colossal print the scheme will fail because people will get confused about the dates, which are perfectly idiotic'. And he knew how to make use of popular clichés about himself. When the Theatre Guild produced *Jitta's Atonement*, which he adapted from the German of Siegfried Trebitsch, he wrote Lawrence Langner,

> I saw your press communication about the play; but I do not want it suggested that it is 95% Shaw and 5% Trebitsch. Novelty is always valuable; and novelty is the one quality that I have lost hopelessly with the affirmation of my reputation. The line to take is to boom Trebitsch . . . and to suggest that as what has been lacking in my plays is HEART, the combination of the emotional Trebitsch with the intellectual Shaw is ideal, and will make the most dramatic event of the season.[26]

Shaw was not only concerned with getting an audience into the theatre: he felt responsible for their comfort once they got there. During the run of *John Bull's Other Island* at the Court, he wrote to Vedrenne:

> [William] Archer came into my box today because he couldnt stand the cold in the stalls. Four cases of frostbite were treated at the Chelsea infirmary – one stall & three pit. A man in the dress circle got so rheumatic after the second act that he had to be lifted out by the attendants. The Morning Post has lumbago for life. The Daily Mail threatens to head his article 'A Frost at The Court'. The fireman caught one man attempting to set fire to the theatre. You will have to warm the theatre and to announce the fact in the advertisements, or the Christmas piece is done for.
>
> There is not a hook or a hat peg in the boxes. You can get excellent ones for threepence apiece. The man in Box B said

26 Letters: to Granville Barker, Sept. 27, 1903, in *Shaw-Barker*, p. 20; to Lawrence Langner, Sept. 30, 1922, in Langner, *G.B.S.*, p. 95.

that if there had been a hook he would have hanged himself to draw public attention to the frightful cold. My wife was affected to tears by the play; and her tears froze so that it took me five minutes to get her eyes open with the warmth of my hands, which are now covered with chilblains. My mother went to sleep; and we are still (6.15) vainly trying to wake her. I think you have done for her. You can get coals & blankets at the Parish Hall, I believe. Why not apply?[27]

Shaw's ideal theatre would not only be adequately heated, it would have superior optics and acoustics. The seating accommodations would be comfortable, in contrast to the present state of affairs: 'If criminals were crowded together in our prisons without proper ventilation and elbow room, as playgoers are in our theatres, there would be an agitation against the cruelty of the authorities.' Each seat would be wide enough for comfort, and there would be enough space between rows so that one could walk through without falling into the laps of those seated. If a good play makes the theatre-goer forget his discomfort, a bad play makes him remember it and hesitate to attend the theatre the next time. In Shaw's ideal theatre, plush and velvet upholstery would be abolished in favour of cushions covered with woollen cloth. This theatre, moreover, would be beautiful: '. . . a theatre which is panelled, and mirrored, and mantelpieced like the first-class saloon of a Peninsular and Oriental liner or a Pullman drawing room car, is no place for Julius Caesar, or indeed for anything except tailor-made drama and farcical comedy.' A theatre should make the playgoer feel that he is in 'a place where high scenes are to be enacted and dignified things to be done'. Such 'petty cadgings [as] charges for programs and cloakroom fees' would be eliminated. The audience would not be made to feel uncomfortable because they are not fashionably dressed, but would be encouraged to wear what they wear to the cinema. This, Shaw believed, was one reason for the success of motion pictures.[28]

[27] Letter to J. E. Vedrenne, Nov. 26, 1904, Enthoven Collection.
[28] *Our Theatres in the Nineties*, III, 117-9; *Shaw on Theatre*, pp. 135, 177-81.

Shaw understood that some of these reforms were impractical within the contemporary economic framework. For one thing, the large amount of ground space required for the type of seating arrangement he would like was impossible in the West End because of high rents. But, he suggested, there was no reason for the theatre to remain in the West End. If the Church could move from the centre of the city to the suburbs, then so could the theatre. 'It is clear to me that we shall never become a play-going people until we discard our fixed idea that it is the business of the people to come to the theatre, and substitute for it the idea that it is the business of the theatre to come to the people.'[29] The theatre, then, should be decentralized and made as easily accessible to the people as motion picture houses.

Shaw was indeed a 'man of the theatre' – writing plays, casting them, mounting and rehearsing them, putting them before an audience, and getting an audience to sit before them. Convinced that the art of play production was as much his business as the art of playwriting, he had a guiding hand in every aspect of play production. As director, he planned blocking, worked closely with actors during rehearsals, and helped them to polish their performances in order to achieve maximum stage effectiveness. But Shaw was a director, not only an acting coach. Sound-effects, music, lighting, scenery, costumes, and make-up – all elements of play production fell within his directorial jurisdiction as he guided artists in each of these areas to express themselves in ways that would further the total effect of the play. Did he limit the other artists – the actor or designer, for instance? Certainly, inasmuch as any guidance, any control designed to create a unified entity from disparate theatrical elements is limiting. And Shaw, who knew the effects he wanted to achieve, was a strong director. But many artists who worked under his supervision – Lillah McCarthy, Forbes Robertson, Sir Cedric Hardwicke, Joseph Harker, Lee Simonson, among others – felt his guidance to be a help rather than a hindrance. In any case, Shaw supervised

29 *Our Theatres in the Nineties*, II, 68-70.

every area of production in trying to realize the play on stage. He had a vision of what the theatre should be, and a willingness to wrestle with the theatre as it was to help him fulfill this vision. Few were as completely immersed in the total theatrical mechanism as Shaw was. One thinks also of Molière and Brecht in this regard: playwrights whose comedies reflect social realities, men engaged in the day-to-day theatrical activity of line-rehearsals, budgets, blocking, scene painting, and the like. Molière, Brecht, and Shaw all involved themselves in the total production apparatus. It is clear that Shaw was a practical theatre man, a director whose resources included every aspect of theatre.

Figures 8–11. *Arms and the Man* (1894).

Figure 9. 'Man servant (Nicola)'

Figures 8–11. *Arms and the Man* (1894).

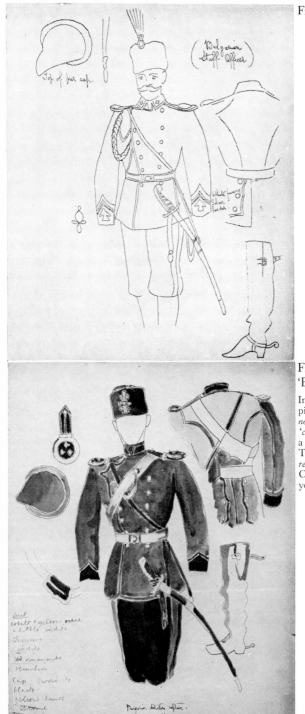

Figure 10. 'Bulgarian staff officer'

Figure 11.
'Bulgarian Artillery captain'.

In the lower left hand portion of the
picture are costume instructions
not in Shaw's hand:
'*coat*   cobalt & yellow ochre
a little indigo
Trousers   indigo
red ornaments   vermilion
Cap. sword. &c. black
yellow bands   chrome'

Bibliography

UNPUBLISHED MATERIAL BY SHAW

A. *Rehearsal Notes*

Arms and the Man
1911 production. Academic Center Library, University of Texas, Austin.

1911 production. British Museum, Add. 50644.

1919 production. Burgunder Collection, Cornell University, Ithaca, N.Y.

1922 production. Burgunder Collection, Cornell University, Ithaca, N.Y.

Undated. Enthoven Collection, Victoria and Albert Museum, London.

Caesar and Cleopatra
1912 production. Academic Center Library, University of Texas, Austin.

Candida
1920 production. British Museum, Add. 50644.

The Doctor's Dilemma
1913 production. Academic Center Library, University of Texas, Austin.

Getting Married
1908 production. Enthoven Collection. Victoria and Albert Museum, London.

Heartbreak House
1921 production. Burgunder Collection, Cornell University, Ithaca, N.Y.
1921 production. British Museum, Add. 50644.
1929 production. British Museum, Add. 50647.

John Bull's Other Island
Undated. Hanley Collection, Academic Center Library, University of Texas, Austin.

Bibliography

Macbeth
 1926 production. British Museum, Add. 50644.

Man and Superman
 1907 production. British Museum, Add. 50735.
 Undated.   British Museum, Add. 50732.

Major Barbara
 1905 production. British Museum, Add. 50733.
 1929 production. British Museum, Add. 50644.
 1935 production. British Museum, Add. 50644.

Misalliance
 1910 production. Hanley Collection, Academic Center Library, University of Texas, Austin.

Pygmalion
 1914 production. Hanley Collection, Academic Center Library, University of Texas, Austin.
 1920 production. British Museum, Add. 50644.

Saint Joan
 1924 production. British Museum, Add. 50644.

You Never Can Tell
 1905 production. British Museum, Add. 50731.
 Undated.   British Museum, Add. 50734.
 Undated.   Academic Center Library, University of Texas, Austin.

B. *Letters Quoted or Paraphrased*

To the *B.B.C.*, in Burgunder Collection, Cornell University, Ithaca, N.Y.:
 May 27, 1941.
 Sept. 1, 1941.

To *Boulton, Matthew*, in The Philbrick Library, Los Altos Hills, Calif.:
 Sept. 1, 1929.

To *Browne, Maurice*, in Hanley Collection, Academic Center Library, University of Texas, Austin:
 March 17, 1915.

To *Champion, H. H.*, in Hanley Collection, Academic Center Library, University of Texas, Austin:
 Dec. 14, 1911.

To *Charrington, Charles,* in British Museum, Add. 50532:
    March 4, 1900 (copy of letter).
    April 15, 1900 (copy of letter).

To *Craig, Edith,* in Burgunder Collection, Cornell University, Ithaca, N.Y.:
    July 17, 1940 (draft of letter).

To *Fagan, J. B.,* in Burgunder Collection, Cornell University, Ithaca, N.Y.:
    Oct. 20, 1921.

To *Faversham, William,* in Hanley Collection, Academic Center Library, University of Texas, Austin.
    April 7, 1916.
    Aug. 3, 1916.
    April 19, 1917.
    Dec. 9, 1917.
    Undated.

To *Forbes-Robertson, Sir Johnston,* in British Museum, Add. 50534:
    Dec. 20, 1903 (draft of letter).

To *Martin-Harvey, Sir John,* in Houghton Library, Harvard College, Cambridge, Mass.:
    Nov. 26, 1926.
    Oct. 9, 1930.

To *Hiller, Wendy,* courtesy Miss Hiller:
    Aug. 17, 1936 (copy of letter).

To *Irving, Laurence,* in Houghton Library, Harvard College, Cambridge, Mass.:
    Dec. 26, 1900.

To *Lewis, Cecil,* in Berg Collection, New York Public Library:
    April 18, 1932.

To *Rehan, Ada,* in Hanley Collection, Academic Center Library, University of Texas, Austin:
    Aug. 30, 1904.

To *Russell, Annie,* in Manuscript Room, New York Public Library:
    Nov. 20, 1905.
    Nov. 27, 1905.

To *Shine, John L.,* in Hanley Collection, Academic Center Library, University of Texas, Austin:
    Oct. 29, 1904.

Bibliography

To *Stephens, Yorke,* in Enthoven Collection, Victoria and Albert Museum, London:
 May 21, 1900.

To *Terry, Ellen,* in The Philbrick Library, Los Altos Hills, Calif.:
 Jan. 31, 1897.

To *Trebitsch, Siegfried,* in Berg Collection, New York Public Library:
 Dec. 10, 1902.
 Dec. 18, 1902.
 Jan. 10, 1903.
 Feb. 14, 1903.
 Aug. 10, 1903.
 June 16, 1904.
 Dec. 13, 1904.
 May 7, 1906.
 June 18, 1906.
 Aug. 18, 1906.
 Nov. 21, 1907.
 Jan. 29, 1913.
 April 19, 1921.
 Nov. 29, 1929.
 Dec. 19, 1929.

To *Vedrenne, J. E.,* in Enthoven Collection, Victoria and Albert Museum, London:
 Nov. 26, 1904.
 Jan. 10, 1906.

To *Vedrenne, J. E.,* in Hanley Collection, Academic Center Library, University of Texas, Austin:
 Oct. 26, 1904.
 April 6, 1908.
 April 26, 1908.

To *Welsh, James,* in Berg Collection, New York Public Library:
 Jan. 30, 1899.

C. *Illustrations.* (Except as noted, in Hanley Collection, Academic Center Library, University of Texas, Austin.)

Arms and the Man, costume sketches: Bluntschli, Nicola, Petkoff, Sergius. British Museum, Add. 50603.

The Devil's Disciple, sketches, plans, and instructions for French production: ground plan, Act I; perspective sketch, Act I; ground plan, Act II; perspective sketch, Act II; ground plan, Act III, Scenes 1, 2, and 3.

Misalliance, ground plan.

Misalliance, perspective sketch.

D. *Typescripts of Plays*

'Arms and the Man', 1894. Yale University Library, New Haven, Conn.

'Candida', 1895. University of California at Los Angeles.

'Major Barbara', 1905. Houghton Library, Harvard College, Cambridge, Mass.

E. *Notes in Margins of Published Plays*

Arms and the Man. British Museum, Add. 50602.

Caesar and Cleopatra, British Museum, Add. 50611.

Mrs Warren's Profession, British Museum, Add. 50600.

The Philanderer, British Museum, Add. 50597.

Pygmalion, British Museum, Add. 50639.

F. *Miscellaneous*

Caesar and Cleopatra, 'Exclamations and Interruptions for Extra Ladies and Gentlemen with Cues'. Hanley Collection, Academic Center Library, University of Texas, Austin.

Caesar and Cleopatra, 'Notes to Act I'. Berg Collection, New York Public Library.

Captain Brassbound's Conversion, 'Dialogue for the five extras representing Brassbound's crew'. Hanley Collection, Academic Center Library, University of Texas, Austin.

The Devil's Disciple, Property List. Hanley Collection, Academic Center Library, University of Texas, Austin.

The Devil's Disciple, sketch of fireplace, Acts I and II. Hanley Collection, Academic Center Library, University of Texas, Austin.

Draft of an Agreement, between Shaw and Johnston Forbes-Robertson, 1900. Hanley Collection, Academic Center Library, University of Texas, Austin.

————, between Shaw and Richard Mansfield, 1894. Berg Collection, New York Public Library.

Financial Records. Hanley Collection, Academic Center Library, University of Texas, Austin; and British Museum, Add. 50649 and 50731.

Inscription, undated, in *The Tragedie of Hamlet*, ed. John Dover Wilson (Weimar: Cranach Press, 1930). Hanley Collection, Academic Center Library, University of Texas, Austin.

John Bull's Other Island, 'Instructions to the Producer'. British Museum, Add. 50615.

Memorandum of an Agreement, between Shaw and Mrs Virginia Compton, 1918. Yale University Library, New Haven, Conn.

————, between Shaw and Robert Loraine, 1905. Hanley Collection, Academic Center Library, University of Texas, Austin.

————, between Shaw and Roy Limbert, 1938. Berg Collection, New York Public Library.

Notes on back of ticket to British Museum Reading Room. Academic Center Library, University of Texas, Austin.

'Proposed Diploma in Dramatic Art', June 25, 1922. Hanley Collection, Academic Center Library, University of Texas, Austin.

Publicity Release (draft) for *Arms and the Man*, 1911. British Museum, Add. 50644.

Pygmalion, Act I, Sketch and Working Drawing. Hanley Collection, Academic Center Library, University of Texas, Austin.

Reply, undated, in margin of letter-questionnaire dated March 15, 1930, sent by Floryan Sobieniowski. Hanley Collection, Academic Center Library, University of Texas, Austin.

'The Voice', Berg Collection, New York Public Library.

UNPUBLISHED LETTERS BY OTHERS

Granville Barker to Neville Lytton, Oct. 12, 1906. Berg Collection, New York Public Library.

Ronald Gow to author, July 12, 1964.

Wendy Hiller to author, July 12, 1964.

PUBLISHED WORKS BY SHAW

A. The following books are in the Standard Edition of the Works of Bernard Shaw (London: Constable). The year following the work's title represents the first publication in the Standard Edition. After each volume of plays I indicate the names of those plays cited in this study, together with the years of completion, first performance, and first publication. For the collection of *Major Critical Essays*, I cite each essay as well as the year it was first published.

Androcles and the Lion. Overruled. Pygmalion. 1931.

   Androcles and the Lion: completed 1912; first performance 1913; first publication 1914.

   Pygmalion: completed 1913; first performance 1913; first publication 1914.

Back to Methuselah A Metabiological Pentateuch. 1931.

   Back to Methuselah: completed 1920, first performance 1922; first publication 1921.

The Black Girl in Search of God and some lesser tales. 1934.

Cashel Byron's Profession. 1932.

The Doctor's Dilemma, Getting Married, & The Shewing-up of Blanco Posnet. 1932.

   The Doctor's Dilemma: completed 1906; first performance 1906; first publication 1911.

   Getting Married: completed 1908; first performance 1908; first publication 1911.

   The Shewing-up of Blanco Posnet: completed 1909; first performance 1909; first publication 1911.

Geneva, Cymbeline Refinished, & Good King Charles. 1946.

   Cymbeline Refinished: completed 1937; first performance 1937; first publication 1946.

Heartbreak House. 1931.

   Heartbreak House: completed 1919; first performance 1920; first publication 1919.

Bibliography

Annajanska, the Bolshevik Empress: completed 1917; first performance 1918; first publication 1919.

John Bull's Other Island with How He Lied to Her Husband and Major Barbara. 1931.

John Bull's Other Island: completed 1904; first performance 1904; first publication 1907.

Major Barbara: completed 1905; first performance 1905; first publication 1907.

London Music in 1888-89 as Heard by Corno di Bassetto (Later Known as Bernard Shaw) with Some Further Autobiographical Particulars. 1937.

Love Among the Artists. 1932.

Major Critical Essays. 1932.

'The Quintessence of Ibsenism': 1891.

'The Perfect Wagnerite': 1898.

'The Sanity of Art': 1895.

Man and Superman. A Comedy and a Philosophy. 1931.

Man and Superman: completed 1903; first performance 1905; first publication 1903.

Misalliance, The Dark Lady of the Sonnets, & Fanny's First Play. 1932.

Misalliance: completed 1910; first performance 1910; first publication 1914.

The Dark Lady of the Sonnets: completed 1910; first performance 1910; first publication 1910.

Fanny's First Play: completed 1911; first performance 1911; first publication 1914.

Music in London, 1890-1894, 3 vols. 1932.

Our Theatres in the Nineties, 3 vols. 1932.

Pen Portraits and Reviews. 1932.

Plays Pleasant and Unpleasant, 2 vols. 1931.

Vol. I—*Plays Unpleasant:*

Widowers' Houses: completed 1892; first performance 1892; first publication 1893.

The Philanderer: completed 1893; first performance 1905; first publication 1898.

Mrs Warren's Profession: completed 1894; first performance 1905; first publication 1898.

Vol. II—*Plays Pleasant:*

Arms and the Man: completed 1894: first performance 1894; first publication 1898.

Candida: completed 1895; first performance 1897; first publication 1898.

The Man of Destiny: completed 1895; first performance 1897; first publication 1898.

You Never Can Tell: completed 1896; first performance 1899; first publication 1898.

Saint Joan A Chronicle and The Apple Cart A Political Extravaganza. 1932.

Saint Joan: completed 1923; first performance 1923; first publication 1924.

The Apple Cart: completed 1929; first performance 1929; first publication 1930.

The Simpleton, The Six, and The Millionairess. 1936.

The Simpleton of the Unexpected Isles: completed 1934; first performance 1935; first publication 1936.

The Millionairess: completed 1935; first performance 1936; first publication 1936.

Sixteen Self Sketches. 1949.

Three Plays for Puritans. The Devil's Disciple, Caesar and Cleopatra, and Captain Brassbound's Conversion. 1931.

The Devil's Disciple: completed 1897; first performance 1897; first publication 1900.

Caesar and Cleopatra: completed 1898; first performance 1901; first publication 1900.

Captain Brassbound's Conversion: completed 1899; first performance 1900; first publication 1900.

Bibliography

Translations and Tomfooleries. 1932.

    Jitta's Atonement: completed 1922; first performance 1923; first publication 1926.

    The Admirable Bashville: completed 1901; first performance 1902; first publication 1901.

    Passion, Poison, and Petrifaction: completed 1905; first performance 1905; first publication 1905.

B. The following works, entirely or partly by Shaw, are not in the Standard Edition:

Advice to a Young Critic. Ed. E. J. West. New York: Crown, 1955.

Bernard Shaw and Mrs Patrick Campbell: Their Correspondence. Ed. Alan Dent. New York: Knopf, 1952.

Bernard Shaw's Letters to Granville Barker. Ed. C. B. Purdom. London: Phoenix House, 1956.

'Bernard Shaw to Gilbert Murray', *Drama*, n.s., XLII (Autumn 1956), 24-8.

Caesar and Cleopatra. London: Grant Richards, 1904.

Collected Letters, 1874-1897. Ed. Dan H. Laurence. New York: Dodd, Mead, 1965.

Ellen Terry and Bernard Shaw: A Correspondence. Ed. Christopher St. John. New York: The Fountain Press, 1931.

[Farr, Florence, Bernard Shaw, and W. B. Yeats.] *Letters.* Ed. Clifford Bax. New York: Dodd, Mead, 1942.

'George Bernard Shaw as a Man of Letters: The Correspondence with Which He Enlivened the Beginnings of "Major Barbara"', *The New York Times*, Dec. 5, 1915, Sec. VI, p. 6.

'Granville-Barker', *Drama*, n.s., III (Winter 1946), 7-14.

Heartbreak House, Great Catherine, and *Playlets of the War.* London: Constable, 1919.

How to Become a Musical Critic. Ed. Dan H. Laurence. New York: Hill and Wang, 1961.

'In the Picture-Galleries', *Modern Drama*, II (Fall 1959), 150-9.

Letters from George Bernard Shaw to Miss Alma Murray (Mrs Alfred Forman). Edinburgh: Printed for Private Circulation, 1927.

The Matter with Ireland. Ed. David H. Grene and Dan H. Laurence. London: Hart-Davis, 1962.

More Letters from George Bernard Shaw to Miss Alma Murray (Mrs. Alfred Forman). Edinburgh: Printed for Private Circulation, 1932.

The Philanderer. London: Constable, 1906.

Platform and Pulpit. Ed. Dan H. Laurence. New York: Hill and Wang, 1961.

Plays: Unpleasant. London: Grant Richards, 1900.

Pygmalion: A Play in Five Acts: By a Fellow of the Royal Society of Literature [rehearsal edition]. London: Constable, 1913. University of North Carolina Library.

'Qualifications of the Complete Actor', *Dramatic Review*, Sept. 19, 1885. British Museum, Add. 50691.

Review of *How to Develop General Vocal Power*, name of periodical not indicated, Nov. 12, 1886. British Museum, Add. 50692.

The Shaw Alphabet Edition of Androcles and the Lion. Harmondsworth: Penguin, 1962.

Shaw on Shakespeare. Ed. Edwin Wilson. New York: Dutton, 1961.

Shaw on Theatre. Ed. E. J. West. New York: Hill and Wang, 1959.

To a Young Actress: The Letters of Bernard Shaw to Molly Tompkins. Ed. Peter Tompkins. New York: Potter, 1960.

PUBLISHED WORKS BY OTHERS

Armstrong, William A. 'George Bernard Shaw: The Playwright as Producer', *Modern Drama*, VIII (February 1966), 347-61.

Bentley, Eric. *Bernard Shaw, 1856-1950*. New York · New Directions, 1957.

Bishop, G. W. *Barry Jackson and the London Theatre*. London: Barker, 1933.

Casson, Sir Lewis. 'A Remembrance', in *Setting the Stage: A Guidebook to Season '66: The Minnesota Theatre Company, Fourth Season*. Minneapolis: Tyrone Guthrie Theatre, 1966.

Bibliography

Chappelow, Allan (ed.). *Shaw the Villager and Human Being*. London: Skilton, 1961.

Deans, Marjorie. *Meeting at the Sphinx: Gabriel Pascal's Production of Bernard Shaw's Caesar and Cleopatra*. London: Macdonald, n.d.

Desmond MacCarthy's The Court Theatre 1904-1907: A Commentary and Criticism. Ed. Stanley Weintraub. Coral Gables, Fla.: University of Miami Press, 1966.

Dunbar, Janet. *Mrs G.B.S.* London: Harrap, 1963.

Forbes-Robertson, Sir Johnston. *A Player Under Three Reigns*. Boston: Little, Brown, 1925.

Hardwicke, Cedric. *Let's Pretend: Recollections and Reflections of a Lucky Actor*. London: Grayson and Grayson, 1932.

―――― (as told to James Brough). *A Victorian in Orbit*. Garden City, N.Y.: Doubleday, 1961.

Harker, Joseph. *Studio and Stage*. London: Nisbet, 1924.

Harris, Frank. *Bernard Shaw*. Garden City, N.Y.: Garden City Publishing Co., 1931.

Henderson, Archibald. *George Bernard Shaw: Man of the Century*. New York: Appleton-Century-Crofts, 1956.

――――. 'George Bernard Shaw Self-Revealed', *The Fortnightly Review*, n.s., CCIX (April, May 1926), 433-42, 610-18.

――――. *Table-Talk of G.B.S.* New York: Harper, 1925.

Jones, Doris Arthur. *Taking the Curtain Call: The Life and Letters of Henry Arthur Jones*. New York: Macmillan, 1930.

Langner, Lawrence. *G.B.S. and the Lunatic*. New York: Atheneum, 1963.

Loewenstein, F. E. *The Rehearsal Copies of Bernard Shaw's Plays*. London: Reinhardt and Evans, 1950.

Loraine, Winifred. *Head Wind: The Story of Robert Loraine*. New York: William Morrow, n.d.

Mander, Raymond, and Joe Mitchenson. *Theatrical Companion to Shaw*. London: Rockliff, 1954.

Maude, Cyril. *Lest I Forget*. New York: Sears, 1928.

McCarthy, Lillah. *Myself and My Friends.* New York: Dutton, 1933.

Meisel, Martin. *Shaw and the Nineteenth-Century Theater.* Princeton, N.J.: Princeton University Press, 1963.

Pearson, Hesketh. *G.B.S.: A Postscript.* New York, Harper: 1950.

Ricketts, Charles. *Self-Portrait.* Collected and Compiled by T. Sturge Moore. Ed. Cecil Lewis. London: Peter Davies, 1939.

Rosset, B. C. *Shaw of Dublin: The Formative Years.* University Park: Pennsylvania State University Press, 1964.

Simonson, Lee. *Part of a Lifetime.* New York: Duell, Sloan and Pearce, 1943.

Vanbrugh, Irene. *To Tell My Story.* London: Hutchinson, 1950.

INDEX

Index